Super Review®

All You Need to Know!

PSYCHOLOGY I

By the Staff of
Research & Education Association
Dr. M. Fogiel, Director

Research & Education Association
61 Ethel Road West
Piscataway, New Jersey 08854

SUPER REVIEW®
OF PSYCHOLOGY I

Year 2003 Printing

Printed in the United States of America

Library of Congress Control Number 00-133919

International Standard Book Number 0-87891-089-1

REA's Books Are The Best...
They have rescued lots of grades and more!

(a sample of the hundreds of letters REA receives each year)

" Your books are great! They are very helpful, and have upped my grade in every class. Thank you for such a great product. "

Student, Seattle, WA

" Your book has really helped me sharpen my skills and improve my weak areas. Definitely will buy more. "

Student, Buffalo, NY

" Compared to the other books that my fellow students had, your book was the most useful in helping me get a great score. "

Student, North Hollywood, CA

" I really appreciate the help from your excellent book. Please keep up your great work. "

Student, Albuquerque, NM

" Your book was such a better value and was so much more complete than anything your competition has produced (and I have them all)! "

Teacher, Virginia Beach, VA

(more on next page)

(continued from previous page)

"Your books have saved my GPA, and quite possibly my sanity. My course grade is now an 'A', and I couldn't be happier."

Student, Winchester, IN

"These books are the best review books on the market. They are fantastic!"

Student, New Orleans, LA

"Your book was responsible for my success on the exam. . . I will look for REA the next time I need help."

Student, Chesterfield, MO

"I think it is the greatest study guide I have ever used!"

Student, Anchorage, AK

"I encourage others to buy REA because of their superiority. Please continue to produce the best quality books on the market."

Student, San Jose, CA

"Just a short note to say thanks for the great support your book gave me in helping me pass the test . . . I'm on my way to a B.S. degree because of you !"

Student, Orlando, FL

WHAT THIS **Super Review** WILL DO FOR YOU

This **Super Review** provides all that you need to know to do your homework effectively and succeed on exams and quizzes.

The book focuses on the core aspects of the subject, and helps you to grasp the important elements quickly and easily.

Outstanding **Super Review** features:

- Topics are covered in logical sequence

- Topics are reviewed in a concise and comprehensive manner

- The material is presented in student-friendly language that makes it easy to follow and understand

- Individual topics can be easily located

- Provides excellent preparation for midterms, finals and in-between quizzes

- In every chapter, reviews of individual topics are accompanied by Questions **Q** and Answers **A** that show how to work out specific problems

- At the end of most chapters, quizzes with answers are included to enable you to practice and test yourself to pinpoint your strengths and weaknesses

- Written by professionals and test experts who function as your very own tutors

Dr. Max Fogiel
Program Director

CONTENTS

CHAPTER 1

Introduction to Psychology

1.1 Defining Psychology and Psychologists

Psychology is the scientific study of behavioral and mental processes. Psychologists study both human and animal behavior as well as **overt** (external and observable) and **covert** (internal and nonobservable) behaviors.

The **goals of psychology** are to

(1) describe behavior,

(2) predict behavior,

(3) explain behavior, and

(4) control behavior.

Psychologists have either doctoral or master's-level degrees. A **doctoral degree** (Ph.D., Psy.D., or Ed.D.) is received after three to six years of post-undergraduate training in psychology. A **master's degree** (M.S. or M.A.) is granted after one to three years of post-undergraduate training in psychology. Some areas of psychological training at both the doctoral and master's degree levels require an additional year of **internship** or **on-the-job** training in a clinic, hospital, school, prison, or business setting.

Problem Solving Example:

 What is psychology?

Broadly defined, psychology is the study of the behavior of living organisms. Most psychologists today agree with this definition, although many expand upon it. Some psychologists further describe it as the study of experience – that which occurs inside an individual which may or may not be reported by him/her. Other psychologists object to such an inclusion. They believe that inner experience is too subjective to be studied with scientific laws. The existence of such varied approaches adds to the complexity of the field.

Psychology has acquired a multitude of definitions throughout its history. At one time, it was considered to be the study of the mind. However, this definition was changed when it was agreed that the mind is not entirely open to scientific analysis. The workings of the mind can only be known through the observation of the behavior it controls. Recent efforts to make the discipline more objective and scientific have resulted in the definition of psychology as the study of behavior. The next step in understanding psychology is to define behavior.

Behavior refers to any observable action or reaction of a living organism. Psychology is the study of several levels of behavior, each of which is of special interest to various types of psychologists. For example, some psychologists focus on the behavior or actions of nerve cells, sweat glands, and adrenal glands. Other psychologists concentrate on behaviors that exist on a higher level such as aggression, prejudice, or problem solving. Thus the field of psychology is complicated by its several subspecialties, each of which has its own set of approaches.

A key word in the definition of behavior is "observable." Behavior refers to movement, activity, or action that is overt. Some behaviors are more easily observed than others.

An EEG machine is needed to observe brain wave movement, whereas aggressive behavior can be witnessed with the naked eye.

To explain and understand behavior accurately, one must go beyond the mere reporting of observable movement. Four fundamental characteristics must be taken into account. These are: the organism, motivation, knowledge and competence. Differences in behavior are explained in terms of differences in one of these factors. The first factor, the organism, refers to the living biological entity – a human being or lower animal – and its biological characteristics and limits. Behavior cannot be studied properly without accounting for the organism's biological capacity. Its nervous system, endocrine system and other biological structures must be examined. Knowledge of its biological history and heredity are also necessary.

Motivation must also be accounted for in the study of behavior. Motivation is the immediate cause of behavior. Psychologists define it as the immediate forces that act to energize, direct, sustain, and stop a behavior. To understand behavior, we must examine its motivational underpinnings.

In psychology, the word "cognition" is often used in place of "knowledge" – that is, what the organism knows. To examine a particular behavior in its proper perspective, one needs to understand the organism's perception of his environment as well as what he knows, thinks, and remembers.

Competence is the fourth factor necessary in the understanding of behavior. Competence refers to the skills and abilities of an organism – how well he/she can perform a certain task.

Psychology is not as simple as it first appeared. The science of behavior is very complex. Psychologists today need a basic understanding of other scientific fields, such as biology, physics, chemistry and linguistics. In studying psychology, one will also encounter sociology, anthropology, economics, political science and the other social sciences. To thoroughly evaluate behavior, the psychologist must be familiar with all of these areas.

1.2 Major Subfields of Psychology Today

While in graduate school, psychologists are trained and usually specialize in one major subfield of psychology.

The majority of psychologists are either **Clinical** or **Counseling Psychologists**, who study the causes, treatments, and diagnoses of behavioral, emotional, and mental health problems.

Cognitive Psychologists study internal thinking, such as the processing of information, memory, and concept formation.

Comparative Psychologists study and compare behaviors across different species of animals, including humans.

Developmental Psychologists study age-related changes in behavior from the prenatal period through old age. (Some examples include the study of how memory, language, or cognitive behaviors change with age.)

Educational Psychologists work on school-related issues such as designing curricula, teaching, or counseling methods that can be used in the schools.

Experimental Psychologists rely on scientific methods to conduct research in such areas as learning, memory, and sensation and perception.

Industrial or Organizational Psychologists generally work in business or industry on such problems as optimum working conditions, team building, selecting employees, and marketing products.

School Psychologists work directly with students, teachers, or parents in the school setting. School psychologists test, counsel, and make recommendations about individual students who are referred because of learning, emotional, or behavioral concerns.

Social Psychologists study all aspects of social behavior and how people interact with other people. For instance, they study aggressive behavior, helping behavior, friendship formation, etc.

1.3 Historical Approaches to the Study of Psychology

Wilhelm Wundt (1832-1920) began the first experimental psychology laboratory in 1879 at the University of Leipzig, Germany. This occurred as a result of the merger of **philosophy** (questioning truth) and **physiology** (scientific analysis of living organisms). Wundt studied **introspection,** the careful analysis of one's own conscious experiences. Since 1879 there have been several historical approaches to the study of psychology:

Historical Approach (Associated names)	Description
Structuralism Edward Titchener (English, 1867-1927)	Examined the structure of the mind, analyzed structure and content of mental states by introspection, and was concerned with reducing experience to its basic parts.
Functionalism William James (American, 1842-1910)	Proposed the study of how the mind adapts us to our environment. Influenced by Charles Darwin's theories of evolution and natural selection. Felt conscious experience is adaptive and always changing.
Behaviorism Ivan Pavlov (Russian, 1849-1936) John B. Watson (American, 1878-1958) B. F. Skinner (American, 1904-1990)	Stressed the study of observable behavior, not unobservable consciousness. Behavior is assumed to be wholly determined by environmental factors.
Psychoanalysis Sigmund Freud (Austrian, 1856-1939)	Emphasized the study of unconscious mental processes; argued that people are driven by sexual urges and that most emotional conflicts date back to early childhood experiences.
Gestalt Max Wertheimer (German, 1880-1943)	Emphasized perception and that stimuli are perceived as whole entities rather than parts put together ("The whole may be greater than the sum of its parts.")

Humanistic Carl Rogers (American, 1902-1987) Abraham Maslow (American, 1908-1970)	Stressed that humans have enormous potential for personal growth. Emphasized importance of free will, the human ability to make choices, and the uniqueness of the individual.
Cognitive Jean Piaget (Swiss, 1896-1980)	Studied internal, mental representations that are used in perceiving, remembering, thinking and understanding.

Problem Solving Example:

 Discuss the influence of the five early schools of thought on modern psychology.

 The early schools of thought were important in the development of psychology, but today they have largely disappeared. Few psychologists today would identify themselves as belonging to one particular school, although some have certain biases toward one school, especially when there are alternative theories of explanation regarding a particular phenomenon. But despite the biases, practically all psychologists agree that each school had some beneficial effect on the shaping of psychology as we know it today.

Structuralism was criticized severely by the schools of thought which followed it, but structuralist-type ideas are still found in modern psychology. The famous Swiss psychologist Jean Piaget described changes with age in the structure of the human mind. American experimental psychologists examine how knowledge is organized and describe the structure of memory, by which an individual can recall events. In addition, the principles of association which the structuralists used to describe the formation of complex mental events from simpler elements is still the basis of one of today's learning theories.

The most important contribution of functionalism was the emphasis of learning as an important adaptive process. While functionalism was not a coherent school, its principles were important in stressing the functional or pragmatic significance of the mind.

Behaviorism and gestalt psychology have had the greatest influence on the shaping of modern psychology. The behavioristic concept of learned responses as the building blocks of behavior remains an important principle in modern psychological theory. B.F. Skinner is the most well-known behaviorist today. He has developed both a theory based on this basic behavioristic concept and a method of changing behavior-behavior modification. These are based on his observation of the effects of reward and punishment on behavior.

The most influential concept of gestalt psychology is the idea that behavior is a continuous, organizational process, the whole of which is different from the sum of its parts. The preference for process analysis over content analysis of behavior is a gestaltist idea that still has a bearing on many aspects in psychology, the most notable of which is learning.

Psychoanalytic thought has been the most lasting of the five schools. Several psychologists today hold some of its principles, although its influence on human behavior theory has greatly decreased since the height of Freud's popularity. Psychoanalysis, however, is still important in certain areas of clinical psychology and forms the basis of some psychotherapeutic techniques.

1.4 Research Methods

Psychological research is based on the scientific method. The **scientific method** consists of

(1) defining a research problem,

(2) proposing a hypothesis and making predictions,

(3) designing and conducting a research study,

(4) analyzing the data, and

(5) communicating the results and building theories of behavior.

A **sample** is a subset of a population selected to participate in the study. All of the participants in a research study make up the sample.

A **population** includes all members of a class or set from which a smaller sample may be drawn and about whom the researcher wants to draw conclusions.

A **random sample** is one in which every member of the population being studied has an equal chance of being picked for inclusion in the study.

A **biased sample** occurs when every member of a population does not have an equal chance of being chosen.

A **stratified sample** is one in which every relevant subgroup of the population is randomly selected in proportion to its size.

A **subject** is an individual who is actually participating in the research study.

Replications refer to research studies that are repeated, often under different conditions, in order to assure the reliability of the results.

1.4.1 The Experiment

Psychologists use experiments to determine **cause-and-effect relationships.** A **"true experiment"** requires that the researcher systematically manipulate or control one or more variables, hold the other variables constant, and then observe how the research subjects or participants respond to this manipulation. The variable that is manipulated is called the **independent variable.** The response that is measured after the manipulation of the independent variable is known as the **dependent variable.**

An experiment consists of at least two groups of subjects. The **experimental group** is the group that is exposed to the manipulation of the independent variable. Some experiments have more than one experimental group, meaning there are several manipulations of the independent variable. The **control group** of an experiment is not exposed to manipulation of the independent variable. The responses of subjects in the control group are compared to the responses of subjects in the experimental group(s) in order to determine if the independent variable(s) had any effect on the dependent variable.

Subjects usually are assigned to groups in an experiment based on **random assignment** that ensures that each participant had an equal chance of being assigned to any one of the groups. Random assignment helps guarantee that the groups were similar to one another with respect to important characteristics before the manipulation of the independent variable. When subjects are not randomly assigned to groups, it is referred to as a **quasi-experiment.**

Subject bias occurs when research participants' behavior changes because they know they are being studied or because of their expectations. A **placebo** is an inactive substance given in the place of a drug in psychological research. A **placebo effect** occurs when a participant believes they are experiencing a change due to an administered drug which is really a placebo. **Observer or researcher bias** occurs when the expectations of the researcher influence what is recorded or measured. **Double-blind technique** is used to control for both subject and observer biases. In the double-blind technique, neither the subjects nor the researcher who is measuring the dependent variable know who is assigned to which group in an experiment.

A **single-subject experiment** involves the participation of only one subject. The independent variable is systematically changed over time, and the subject's behavior at one time is compared with the same subject's behavior at another time. In this case, time is used as the control.

Problem Solving Example:

Q What is an experiment?

A An experiment is a test of a theory. A theory is basically a set of coherent and explanatory "laws" that are used to make empirical predictions. In psychology, theories are used to predict behavior. An hypothesis is a generalization derived or deduced from a theory. The hypothesis is usually a verbal statement which makes a prediction. When someone sets out to test an hypothesis he must design a real, practical situation which attempts to test the prediction made by the hypothesis. This is an experiment.

If an experiment fails it means that the prediction made from the hypothesis may be incorrect or at least inaccurate. The theory must then be revised. Actually, it is nearly impossible to unequivocally prove or disprove theories because they can only be tested indirectly, through their postulates. Theories can only at best be supported, never proven. Some theories, like psychoanalysis, are strongly criticized by their opponents on the basis of their untestability. It is probably not possible to design an experiment that will convincingly and effectively test the hypotheses derived from the general theory of psychoanalysis.

The experiment is the crux of scientific psychology. It is probably the only effective way of establishing psychological principles and of gathering data which can tell us something about the human mind. The experiment is an objective research tool that is very valuable; however, this does not mean that it is the only tool. There are many areas of psychology that cannot be explored through experimentation; clinical investigation remains one of the best tools for understanding personality and psychopathology.

1.4.2 Nonexperimental Methods

Nonexperimental methods of research do not include the systematic manipulation of variables by the researcher and thus cannot be used to discuss cause-and-effect relationships.

Correlational research involves measuring two (or more) variables in order to determine if they are related. If the value of one variable increases in value as the other also increases in value, this is known as a **positive correlation**. A **negative correlation** occurs when there is an inverse relationship between the variables measured; as the value of one increases, the value of the other decreases.

A **correlation coefficient** is a number that represents the strength of the relationship between the variables measured. A correlation coefficient can range in value from 0 to 1. A **correlation coefficient of 0** indicates no relationship between the variables measured. A **correlation coefficient of 1** indicates a perfect relationship between the two variables: you can predict one variable perfectly by knowing the value of the other. Therefore, the closer a correlation coefficient is to 1, the stronger the relationship between the variables measured, and the closer a correlation coefficient is to 0, the weaker the relationship. Even if a strong correlational relationship is found, however, cause-and-effect conclusions *cannot* be made because there was no systematic manipulation by the researcher.

Naturalistic observation is a research method that occurs in a natural setting that has not been manipulated by the researcher. The researcher systematically observes and records what occurs in an unobtrusive manner. This is done so that the behavior of the subjects being tested is not altered. **Interobserver reliability** is the amount of agreement between two (or more) observers who simultaneously observe the same event.

A **case study** is an in-depth study of a single subject. It can include interviews, observations, and test results. Typically, this type of research generates ideas for more rigorous research.

The **survey method** of collecting data requires the researcher to ask a group of people about behaviors, thoughts, or opinions. Data is collected through questionnaires or interviews.

Qualitative research design encompasses research that is not quantitative. Patterns in the data are sought to formulate theoretical underpinnings of behavior.

1.4.3 Comparing Research Methods

Method	Strengths	Weaknesses
Experiment	Can measure cause-and-effect relationships. Researcher has control.	Sampling errors. Often hard to generalize to real world.
Correlation	Can study real world behavior. Can determine relationships.	May not determine cause and effect.

Naturalistic Observation	Can gather information in its usual setting as it naturally occurs.	May not determine cause and effect. Observer bias possible.
Case Study	Intensive information can be gathered about individuals.	May not determine cause and effect. May be expensive and time consuming. May not be able togeneralize information gathered. Biased sample possible.
Survey	Large amounts of information can be gathered from many people in a relatively short period of time.	May not determine cause and effect. Biased sample possible. Response bias possible. Survey questions might not be reliable or valid.

Problem Solving Example:

 List and describe the important methods of investigation in psychology.

 Psychologists use several methods to study behavior. The method used depends on the type of behavior under investigation. The major methods of psychology are: the individual case study, naturalistic observation, tests, interviews and surveys, and experimentation.

In the individual case study or the case history method, a single individual is examined intensively in order to examine a problem or issue relevant to that person. This method is often used in the assessment and correction of abnormal behavior patterns. In a case study, the psychologist often uses a number of procedures such as collecting biographical data on the individual, administering psychological tests, and conducting interviews with the subject. Sigmund Freud used the individual case study method of investigation.

Naturalistic observation refers to the systematic observation of a certain event or phenomenon in the environment as it occurs naturally, without any intervention on the part of the investigator. This method is often used in schools when there is a behavior problem in a classroom. The researcher avoids manipulation if he believes that it would adversely affect the basic characteristics of the particular phenomenon. If laboratory investigation interferes with the natural occurrence of the phenomenon, then the psychologist would prefer to witness it in its natural environment. For example, certain behavior patterns of monkeys, such as mating behavior, might differ in a laboratory setting. Hence, the psychologist would try to observe this behavior as it occurs in the monkeys' natural habitat.

Numerous psychological tests have been designed to assess certain aspects of behavior. These tests attempt to measure such factors as intelligence, anxiety, and leadership ability. All of these tests consist of a number of questions. When the test is graded, the person receives a composite score which should reflect his typical behavior in normal circumstances.

As previously stated, the interview is used in conjunction with the case study method. Interviews may be structured or unstructured. Structured interviews, in which individuals are asked to respond to a number of preformulated questions, are most often given when the psychologist wants to collect information from a group of people. An unstructured interview is usually used in the intensive study of an individual. Here the direction of the interview is guided by the individual's responses and the examiner's hypotheses concerning the underlying rationale of these responses.

Surveys are similar to psychological tests and interviews in that individuals are asked to reply to a series of questions or items. In a survey, however, the purpose is not to test or analyze a specific aspect of a person or group. The surveyor wishes to learn an opinion, attitude, or belief on a particular issue(s). Newspapers and public opinion polls conduct surveys to obtain the public consensus on a certain topic(s).

In experimentation, the psychologist examines a specific phenomenon in a controlled laboratory environment. Here, he can rule out all extraneous and distracting variables and manipulate, with precise equipment and procedures, the conditions he wishes to examine.

In experimentation, the researcher examines cause and effect relationships between a changing variable and a certain behavior. For example, if a psychologist wishes to examine the effect of early isolation on social development, he might place a monkey in isolation during the first few years of its life. The monkey would be placed in a controlled environment. The animal would receive everything necessary for physical survival, but it would not come into contact with other monkeys. After a certain number of years, the monkey would be placed in a cage with other monkeys who were not deprived as he was. The psychologist would then note the animal's reactions. Hence, the psychologist is attempting to determine the effect of a variable (early isolation) upon a certain behavior (social interaction).

1.4.4 Ethical Guidelines

The **American Psychological Association (APA)** has published ethical guidelines to follow when conducting psychological research with human subjects. Some important points from these guidelines include:

- Psychologists are responsible for the ethical conduct of research conducted by them or by others under their supervision.
- Psychologists conduct research with due concern for the dignity and welfare of the participants.
- Psychologists inform participants that they are free to participate or to decline to participate or to withdraw from the research at any time.
- Psychologists inform participants of significant factors that may be expected to influence their willingness to participate.
- Psychologists must obtain informed consent from research participants prior to filming or recording them.
- Participants should be fully debriefed following any deception.

- Psychologists inform research participants of their anticipated sharing or further use of personally identifiable research data.

- Psychologists provide a prompt opportunity for participants to obtain appropriate information about the nature, results, and conclusions of the research.

- Psychologists must honor all commitments made to research participants.

- The APA also presents additional guidelines for the **use and care of animals** in research.

Quiz: Introduction to Psychology

1. Psychology is best defined as

    (A) the study of the mind.

    (B) the study of experience.

    (C) the study of behavior.

    (D) the science of mental processes.

2. The modern psychologist needs to have knowledge of

    (A) biology.

    (B) sociology.

    (C) linguistics.

    (D) All of the above.

3. Personnel policy is the concern of the

    (A) social psychologist.

    (B) industrial psychologist.

(C)   educational psychologist.

(D)   experimental psychologist.

4.   Intensive examination of a single individual is the objective of

(A)   the survey.

(B)   naturalistic observation.

(C)   the case study.

(D)   experimentation.

5.   The major advantage of naturalistic observation is that

(A)   causal relationships can be drawn.

(B)   a controlled environment is employed.

(C)   phenomena can be witnessed in their own environment without adverse interference from the investigator.

(D)   All of the above.

6.   The first experimental psychology laboratory was established by

(A)   Gustav Fechner.

(B)   Wilhelm Wundt.

(C)   Sigmund Freud.

(D)   John Watson.

7.   Gestalt psychology focused mainly on problems dealing with

(A)   perception.

(B)   learning.

(C) motivation.

(D) development.

8. The founder of psychoanalysis is

   (A) William James.

   (B) Ivan Pavlov.

   (C) Sigmund Freud.

   (D) Edward Titchender.

9. A _____ sample is one in which every relevant subgroup of the population is randomly selected in proportion to its size.

   (A) stratified

   (B) biased

   (C) free

   (D) total

10. According to the ethical guidelines published by the American Psychological Association (APA), psychologists who are conducting research with humans must

   (A) inform participants of significant factors that may be expected to influence their willingness to participate.

   (B) inform participants that they are free to withdraw from research at any time.

   (C) inform research participants of their anticipated sharing or further use of personally identifiable research data.

   (D) All of the above.

ANSWER KEY

1.	(C)	6.	(B)
2.	(D)	7.	(A)
3.	(B)	8.	(C)
4.	(C)	9.	(A)
5.	(C)	10.	(D)

CHAPTER 2

Biological Basis of Behavior

2.1 The Nervous System

Functions of the nervous system:

(1) Processes incoming information,

(2) Integrates incoming information,

(3) Influences and directs reactions to incoming information.

2.1.1 Divisions of the Nervous System

The nervous system is divided into the **central nervous system** and the **peripheral nervous system:**

Central Nervous System Peripheral Nervous System

Brain Spinal Cord Somatic Autonomic

Sympathetic Parasympathetic

All nerves encased in bone make up the **central nervous system.** The central nervous system is responsible for processing information and directing actions.

The **peripheral nervous system** is made up of all nerves that are not encased in bone, and its main function is to carry messages to and from the central nervous system.

The **somatic division** of the peripheral nervous system carries messages inward to the central nervous system from the sensory organs (by means of **afferent** or **sensory neurons**) and outward from the central nervous system (by means of **efferent** or **motor neurons**) to the muscles for action. A **reflex arc** occurs when an afferent message travels to the spinal cord and an efferent message for action immediately returns to the muscle, bypassing the brain.

The **autonomic division** of the peripheral nervous system is responsible for involuntary functions of the body. This autonomic nervous system is divided into the **sympathetic** (known as the "fight or flight" branch; activates the body for emergencies) and **parasympathetic** (quiets the body and conserves energy) **branches:**

Sympathetic Branch	**Parasympathetic Branch**
Dilates pupils	Constricts pupils
Inhibits tears	Stimulates tears
Inhibits salivation	Increases salivation
Activates sweat glands	Decreases heart rate
Increases heart rate	Constricts blood vessels
Increases respiration	Decreases respiration
Inhibits digestion	Stimulates digestion
Releases adrenaline	Contracts bladder
Stimulates glucose release	Stimulates elimination
Relaxes bladder	Stimulates sexual arousal
Inhibits elimination	
Inhibits genitals	

2.1.2 Neurons

Neurons are specialized cells that transmit information from one part of the body to another. Nerves are bundles of neurons. The **function** of most neurons is to **receive information** from other neurons and to **pass this information on.**

Structural features of neurons:

Soma – The **cell body** of the neuron.

Dendrites – The branching projections of neurons that **receive information** from other neurons and conduct information **toward** the **cell body.**

Axon – The long, thin fiber that **transmits information away from** the cell body of a neuron **toward other neurons.**

Myelin Sheath – An **insulating material** that **encases** some axons and permits **faster transmission** of information. **Prevents** neurons from **communicating randomly.**

Synapse – The small **space** between neurons where communication takes place.

Terminal Buttons – **Small knobs** at the end of axons that **secrete chemicals.**

Synaptic Cleft – A **microscopic gap** between the terminal button of one neuron and the cell membrane of another. The place where chemicals are released.

2.1.3 Communication within the Nervous System

The nervous system is considered an **electrochemical system.** Communication within a neuron is **electrical;** communication between neurons is **chemical.**

Neurons are filled with and surrounded by electrically charged molecules called **ions.** A neuron at rest has an ion distribution that makes the axon more negatively charged than the outside of the nerve cell. **Resting potential** is the stable, negative charge of an inactive neuron and is the term used to describe the difference in electrical potential

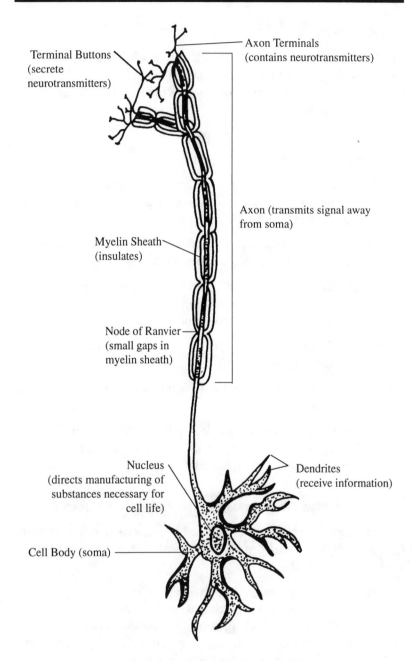

Terminal Buttons
(secrete
neurotransmitters)

Axon Terminals
(contains neurotransmitters)

Axon (transmits signal away
from soma)

Myelin Sheath
(insulates)

Node of Ranvier
(small gaps in
myelin sheath)

Nucleus
(directs manufacturing of
substances necessary for
cell life)

Dendrites
(receive information)

Cell Body (soma)

Figure 2.1 A Typical Nerve Cell

between the outside and the inside of a resting nerve cell. Under these conditions the soma and axon are said to be **polarized.** The brief change in electrical charge that is caused by a dendrite being stimulated or **depolarized** and by the resultant inflow of positively charged sodium ions is called an **action potential.** A **spike** is a nerve impulse generated by the neuron reaching action potential. After the firing of an action potential comes the **refractory period** when no further action potentials can fire.

The firing of a neuron or action potential is an **all or none proposition.** This means that the neuron will fire an action potential of a high magnitude independent of the size of the original stimulus. In other words, if there is no stimulus, there will be no action potential. If there is a stimulus, weak or strong, there will be an action potential.

A neuron passes its message on to another neuron by releasing chemical **neurotransmitters** into the synapse. A **presynaptic neuron** sends the neural message and a **postsynaptic neuron** receives the message. A neurotransmitter can stimulate a postsynaptic neuron only at specific **receptor sites** on its dendrites and soma. Receptor sites respond to only one type of neurotransmitter. This **lock and key model** means that specific neurotransmitters work only at specific kinds of synapses. Neurons that respond to the same neurotransmitter form a **neurotransmitter system.**

Neurotransmitters may **excite** or **inhibit** the next neuron. Stimulation of an **excitatory synapse** makes the neuron more likely to respond; stimulation of an **inhibitory synapse** makes production of an action potential less likely.

Examples of neurotransmitters include:

Neurotrans-mitter (Abbreviation)	Function	Associated Disorders
Acetylcholine (ACh)	Excitatory neurotransmitter related to movement of all muscles as well as arousal, attention, anger, aggression, sexuality and thirst.	Memory loss in patients with Alzheimer's disease.

Dopamine (DA)	Produces both excitatory and inhibitory postsynaptic potentials that control posture and movement.	Parkinson's disease; Schizophrenia
Gama-aminobutyric acid (GABA)	Inhibits central nervous system and regulates anxiety and movement.	Anxiety disorders; Huntington's disease
Glutamate (Glu)	Major excitatory neurons in central nervous system; important for learning and memory.	Memory loss; Alzheimer's disease.
Norepinephrine (NE)	Important for psychological arousal, mood changes, sleep, and learning.	Bipolar mood disorder
Serotonin (5-HT)	Regulates sleep, mood, appetite, and pain.	Depression

Antagonists are drugs that inhibit neurotransmission. **Agonists** are drugs that stimulate neurotransmission.

Endorphins and **neuromodulators** are chemicals that act at the synapse of neurons. Endorphins are **neuropeptides** (made from **amino acids**) and occur naturally in the brain. They decrease a person's sensitivity to pain. **Neuromodulators** do not carry neural messages directly, instead they can either increase or decrease the activity of specific neurotransmitters.

Problem Solving Example:

Distinguish between the central and peripheral nervous systems with respect to their function and location.

The central and peripheral nervous systems can be distinguished in terms of location and basic functions. The central nervous system (or CNS) includes the brain and the spinal cord. The brain is, of course, located within the skull and the spinal cord is encased in the bony spinal column which runs down the center of the back. The peripheral nervous system (PNS), on the other hand, consists of nerve fibers which run from the CNS to the periphery, i.e., the hands, feet, internal organs, etc. It includes all parts of the nervous system not encased in the bony skull and spine.

The CNS and PNS can also be distinguished in terms of function. The PNS serves mainly as a relay route for information travelling between the central nervous system and the rest of the body. It consists basically of two types of nerves. The first includes the afferent nerves which run from the body to the spinal cord. The second type are the motor or efferent nerves which leave the CNS to travel back to the rest of the body.

The CNS functions as an integrative center. This means that it organizes, collates, and stores information sent to it by the PNS. It consists basically of bundles of nerve fibers composed of axons and dendrites, called pathways, and groups of cell bodies called centers. Pathways are specific in that they transmit only certain types of information to the appropriate centers.

The PNS can also perform some integrative activity. This activity occurs in groups of cell bodies called ganglia. The most important integrative centers of the PNS are two series of ganglia located alongside the spinal column. These are the sympathetic ganglia and the sensory or dorsal root ganglia.

2.2   The Brain

Gray matter refers to the neurons in the brain **without myelin.** **White matter** in the brain consists of **myelinated neurons.**

The **cerebral cortex** is the outer surface of the brain surrounding the cerebral hemispheres. It contains small grooves called **sulci** and large grooves called **fissures** and bulges between adjacent sulci or fissures called **gyri.** The cerebral cortex processes all perceptions and

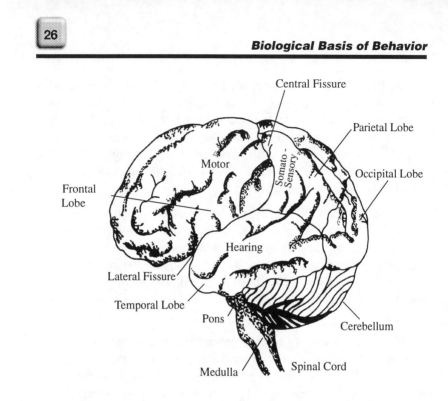

Figure 2.2 Major Areas of the Brain

complex thoughts. In evolutionary terms, it is the most recently developed brain structure.

The brain can be divided into the **hindbrain,** the **midbrain,** and the **forebrain.**

2.2.1 The Hindbrain

The **hindbrain** is located in the bottom portion of the brain and is an extension of the spinal cord. In evolutionary terms, it is the oldest portion of the brain.

The **major components of the hindbrain** are:

Medulla – The oblong structure at the top of the spinal cord that controls many vital life-support functions such as breathing, heart rate, and blood pressure.

Pons – Located above the medulla. Connects the lower brain regions with higher brain regions. The pons is important for sleep, dreaming, and arousal. Pons means "bridge."

Cerebellum – Located at the rear of the brain and controls movement, coordination, balance, muscle tone, and learning motor skills. Resembles a miniature version of the cerebrum.

Reticular Activating System (RAS) – Monitors the general level of activity in the hindbrain and maintains a state of arousal. Keeps the brain awake even during sleep. The RAS is part of the reticular formation, which extends to the upper border of the midbrain.

2.2.2 The Midbrain

The **midbrain** continues upward from the pons portion of the hindbrain and lies between the hindbrain and the forebrain.

The midbrain **relays sensory information** from the spinal cord to the forebrain.

The **upper portion** of the **reticular activating system** is located in the midbrain.

2.2.3 The Forebrain

Not only does the **forebrain** make up the largest part of the brain, it is also the most highly developed portion of the brain.

The **major components of the forebrain** are:

Cerebrum – The largest part of the forebrain and responsible for complex mental activities. Its outer surface is the **cerebral cortex** and is divided into two **cerebral hemispheres.** Contains four major lobes: the **frontal lobe** that controls voluntary movement and includes the **motor cortex;** the **parietal lobe** that contains the primary **somatosensory area** that manages skin senses; the **occipital lobe** is located in the back of the head and contains the **visual cortex;** and the **temporal lobe** contains the **auditory cortex** and is located on each side of the head above the temples.

Limbic System – Related structures that control emotion, motivation, and memory. Contains **amygdala** and **hippocampus.**

Corpus Callosum – Enormous communication network that connects the right and left cerebral hemispheres.

Thalamus – Relays and translates information from all of the senses, except smell, to higher levels in the brain.

Hypothalamus – Plays a major role in the regulation of basic biological drives and controls autonomic functions such as hunger, thirst, and body temperature. Regulates the **pituitary gland.**

2.2.4 Hemispheres of the Brain

The cerebrum is divided into two hemispheres known as the **right** and **left cerebral hemispheres.** The main interconnection between the two hemispheres of the brain is a large set of axons called the **corpus callosum.**

Severe **epilepsy** may be treated by cutting the corpus callosum which results in a **split brain.**

The left hemisphere controls the right side of the body and the right hemisphere controls the left side of the body.

Although both hemispheres are capable of carrying out most tasks, the left hemisphere is often more active in verbal and logical tasks and the right hemisphere usually specializes in spatial, artistic, and musical tasks.

The brain can be monitored using certain devices:

PET scanning (positron emission tomography) creates a visual image of functioning in various parts of the brain by tracing chemical activity.

MRI (magnetic-resonance imaging) scanner is another imaging technique that provides clear pictures of the structural anatomy and chemistry of the brain by passing a strong magnetic field through the person's head.

CAT scan (computerized axial tomography) presents a picture of the human brain by passing X-ray beams through the head at various angles.

EEG (electroencephalograph) records the electrical activity of the brain.

Problem Solving Example:

 What are the three main divisions of the brain? Which major areas does each contain?

 The human brain is considered to have three major divisions; these are the hindbrain, midbrain, and forebrain.

The hindbrain is located at the base of the brain near the beginning of the spinal cord – just above the back of the neck. It contains the major 'primitive' parts of the brain. That is, as man evolved and developed a more complex portion of the brain, this essential portion of the brain stayed much the same, while additional layers were added on to it. The hindbrain includes three major parts – the cerebellum, the pons, and the medulla oblongata. The cerebellum functions in coordinating movements, the pons serves among other functions to connect the two halves of the cerebellum. The medulla is the center for control of breathing and heart rate.

The midbrain lies on top of the hindbrain. It consists of an upper portion called the tectum, and a lower part, the tegmentum. The tectum functions in the visual (sight) and auditory (hearing) systems. The tegmentum contains part of our sleep and arousal system and contains centers for eye movements.

The forebrain is the "highest" portion of the brain, both physically and in degree of complexity. Its major parts include the cerebral cortex, thalamus, hypothalamus, the basil ganglia, and the limbic system.

The cortex and thalamus function in perception, thinking, and learning. The hypothalamus and limbic systems are important in the control of motivation and emotion. The basil ganglia plays a part in motor control, the extrapyramidal motor system, and emotion. The cerebral cortex is the most complex component of the forebrain, and thus of our entire brain. It is the center of most of our higher order cognitive processes.

2.3   Hormones and the Endocrine System

The **endocrine system** is a system of glands that release chemical messengers called **hormones** which are carried by the bloodstream to target organs.

Major glands of the endocrine system:

Gland	Hormones Secreted	Description
Adrenal Cortex	Steroids	Regulates salt and carbohydrate metabolism.
Adrenal Medulla	Adrenaline Noradrenaline	Prepares body for action.
Gonads	Estrogen Progesterone Testosterone	Affects reproductive organs, sexual behavior, and physical development.
Hypothalamus	Neurosecretions	Controls the pituitary gland.
Pancreas	Insulin Glucagon	Regulates sugar metabolism.
Pituitary Gland	Thyrotropin Oxytocin Corticotrophin Prolactin	**Master gland;** controls growth and other glands.
Thyroid Gland	Thyroxine Calcitonin	Regulates metabolism.

Problem Solving Example:

 Define a hormone. How would you go about proving that a particular gland is responsible for a specific function?

The endocrine system constitutes the second great communicating system of the body, with the first being the nervous system. The endocrine system consists of ductless glands which secrete hormones. A hormone is a chemical substance synthesized by a specific organ or tissue and secreted directly into the blood. The hormone is carried via the circulation to other sites of the body where its actions are exerted. Hormones are typically carried in the blood from the site of production to the site(s) of action, but certain hormones produced by neuro-secretory cells in the hypothalamus act directly on their target areas without passing through the blood. The distance travelled by hormones before reaching their target area varies considerably. In terms of chemical structure, hormones generally fall into two categories: steroids and amino acid derivatives. The latter ranges in size from small molecules containing several peptides to very large proteins. Hormones serve to control and integrate many body functions such as reproduction, organic metabolism and energy balance, and mineral metabolism. Hormones also regulate a variety of behaviors, particularly sexual behaviors.

To determine whether a gland is responsible for a particular function or behavior, an investigator usually begins by surgically removing the gland and observing the effect upon the animal. The investigator would then replace the gland with one transplanted from a closely related animal, and determine whether the changes induced by removing the gland can be reversed by replacing it. When replacing the gland, the experimenter must be careful to ensure that the new gland becomes connected with the vascular system of the recipient. This must be done so that secretions from the transplanted gland can enter the blood of the recipient. Finally, the experimenter may make an extract of the gland and purify it to determine its chemical structure. Very often the chemical structure of a substance is very much related to its function. Studying the chemical structure may enable the investigator to deduce a mechanism by which the gland-extract functions on a molecular level. The investigator may also inject the purified gland-extract into an experimental animal devoid of such a gland, and see whether the injection effected replacement of the missing function or behavior. Some hormonal chemicals have additive effects.

The investigator may inject a dosage of the purified gland-extract to an intact animal to observe if there was any augmentation of the particular function or behavior under study.

Quiz: Biological Basis of Behavior

1. All of the following are functions of the sympathetic branch of the autonomic nervous system EXCEPT

    (A) Constricts pupils

    (B) Inhibits tears

    (C) Inhibits salivation

    (D) Increases heart rates

2. The cell body of the neuron is the

    (A) soma.

    (B) dendrites.

    (C) axon.

    (D) synapse.

3. Communication within a neuron is _____ ; communication between neurons is _____ .

    (A) electrical; electrical

    (B) chemical; chemical

    (C) chemical; electrical

    (D) electrical; chemical

4. What neurotransmitter(s) is/are associated with Alzheimer's Disease?

    (A) Acetylcholine

    (B) Glutamate

    (C) Both A and B.

    (D) None of the above.

5. The neurotransmitter that regulates sleep, mood, appetite, and pain is

    (A) glutamate.

    (B) dopamine.

    (C) acetylcholine.

    (D) serotonin.

6. In evolutionary terms, the oldest part of the brain is the

    (A) hindbrain.

    (B) midbrain.

    (C) forebrain.

    (D) There is no oldest part of the brain.

7. The most highly developed portion of the brain is

    (A) hindbrain.

    (B) midbrain.

    (C) forebrain.

    (D) Both (A) and (B).

8. The upper portion of the reticular activating system is located in the

    (A) hindbrain.

    (B) midbrain.

    (C) forebrain.

    (D) Both (B) and (C).

9. The gland that controls the pituitary gland is

    (A) adrenal cortex.

    (B) gonads.

    (C) pancreas.

    (D) hypothalamus.

10. The gland that secretes estrogen, progesterone, and testosterone is

    (A) adrenal cortex.

    (B) gonads.

    (C) pancreas.

    (D) hypothalamus.

ANSWER KEY

1.	(A)	6.	(A)
2.	(A)	7.	(C)
3.	(D)	8.	(B)
4.	(C)	9.	(D)
5.	(D)	10.	(B)

CHAPTER 3

Sensation

3.1 Psychophysics

Psychologists study the senses because we come to know our world primarily through them and what we sense often affects our behavior. Our senses inform us of the **presence of stimuli** or of any **change in a stimulus.** The first experimental psychological techniques were developed for the study of sensation. These techniques were called **psychophysical methods.**

Psychophysics is an area of psychology that examines the relationship between sensory stimuli and individual psychological or behavioral reactions to these stimuli. Psychophysics has been traditionally concerned with detecting thresholds. The smallest amount of a stimulus that can be detected or noticed at least 50 percent of the time is called the **absolute threshold. Difference threshold** or **just noticeable difference (jnd)** measures how much a stimulus must change before it becomes noticeably different.

The study of just noticeable difference thresholds lead to **Weber's Law** which states that the amount of change needed to produce a jnd is a **constant proportion** of the original stimulus intensity. Weber's Law indicated that the more intense the stimulus, the more the stimulus intensity has to be increased before a change is noticed. For example, if music was being played softly, a small increase in sound would be noticeable. If the music was being played loudly, it would require a much greater increase in sound to perceive a difference in volume. Stated mathematically, Weber's Law asserts:

$$\frac{\Delta I}{I} = C$$

where

$$\Delta I = \text{jnd}$$
$$I = \text{stimulus of intensity I}$$
$$C = \text{a constant}$$

Fechner generalized Weber's finding to a broader relationship between sensory and physical intensity. **Fechner's Law** states that constant increases in a sensation produce smaller increases in perceived magnitude:

$$S = k \log I$$

This equation asserts that the magnitude of **sensation, S,** increases in proportion to the **logarithm (log)** of **stimulus intensity, I.**

Signal detection theory is a mathematical model that states that individual expectations, prior knowledge, and response bias influence the probability that a stimulus will be recognized. Signal detection theory does not deal with the concept of thresholds but deals only with varying **probabilities** that a stimulus will be **detected.** It takes into account the willingness of people to guess by determining the probability of a person guessing that there is a stimulus or **signal** present when there actually is one and the probability of a person guessing that there is a signal when there is not one. The person's response will depend on the **criterion** she or he sets for how certain she/he must feel before responding "yes, I detect it."

Problem Solving Example:

 Describe the use of thresholds and their relationship to Weber's Law.

A threshold is basically a boundary which separates the stimuli that elicit one response from the stimuli that elicit a different response. (Many reports of psychophysical studies use the Latin equivalent, limen, instead of threshold).

An example is useful in differentiating among the different types of thresholds. Suppose you present to your subject a low frequency tone through a set of calibrated headphones. If the tone is below a certain frequency (measured in hertz, which will be discussed in 3.3.1), the subject's report is "I don't hear anything." If the tone is continually increased it will eventually reach a frequency where the subject reports "Yes, I hear it." The frequency of the tone has now just crossed the lower threshold. This is also referred to as the stimulus threshold and is abbreviated RL (from the German "Reiz Limen"). If the tone is continued to be increased the subject will report that it is getting higher and higher, and by noting these changes a difference threshold (DL) is established. The DL is also referred to as the just noticeable difference (jnd). The jnd is not merely a fixed value but a percentage of a standard value. This proportion is known as Weber's Law and is simply stated as "a stimulus must be increased by a constant fraction of its value to be just noticeably different." This proportion is symbolized as:

$$\frac{\Delta I}{I} = C$$

in which I symbolizes intensity and Delta I the increase necessary to yield a jnd.

If the tone is continually increased it will eventually reach a level where it cannot be perceived (i.e., a dog whistle). This upper limit is the terminal threshold (TL).

3.2   Vision

The sense of vision is sometimes referred to as our most essential or our **dominant sense.**

3.2.1   Light

Light is the physical stimulus for vision. The **visual spectrum** (light that is visible to the human eye) is made up of various wavelengths of light measured in **nanometers (nm).** A nanometer is one-billionth of a meter, and the visual spectrum varies from 400 nm to about 700 nm. Wavelength determines the first of three perceptual dimensions of light: hue or color. Saturation refers to the purity of the light being perceived. The **amplitude** or height of the wave determines **brightness.**

Problem Solving Example:

 Define light and describe its characteristics. How is it measured? What are its primary sources? Define contour and optic array.

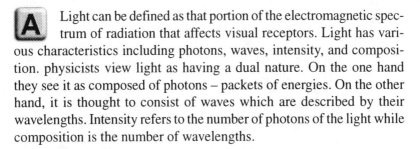 Light can be defined as that portion of the electromagnetic spectrum of radiation that affects visual receptors. Light has various characteristics including photons, waves, intensity, and composition. physicists view light as having a dual nature. On the one hand they see it as composed of photons – packets of energies. On the other hand, it is thought to consist of waves which are described by their wavelengths. Intensity refers to the number of photons of the light while composition is the number of wavelengths.

One device used for measuring light intensity is a photographer's light meter which is capable of transforming physical light energy into a measurable electrical current.

Visible electromagnetic energy; that is, light that can be perceived, comes from a variety of sources – the sun, light bulb, fire. But the most abundant source of light is that which is reflected from object surfaces. Most of the light that enters the eye is reflected light. The brightness of an object – how intense it appears to the perceiver – depends on how much light it receives from a light source and how much is reflected to the perceiver's vision. Light objects reflect almost all the light that illuminates them while dark objects reflect very little since they absorb most of the light that falls on them. Because of the fact that different objects reflect different intensities and wavelengths of light, the human eye can perceive these differences. Contours also make this possible. Contours are the borders between areas that reflect different intensities and wavelengths.

An optic array is a pattern of energy that is reflected from the surface of an object. An array is best illustrated by thinking of an object with visible lines or rays projecting from it from every possible surface point to the eye of the perceiver.

3.2.2   Structure of the Eye

Figure 3.1 shows the structure of the human eye.

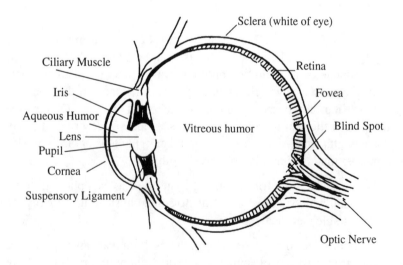

Figure 3.1: Structure of the Human Eye

When light enters the eye, it travels the following path:

Cornea

The transparent outer bulge in front of the eye.

↓

Pupil

The dark circle in the center of the iris of the eye. The **iris** is the colored muscle that surrounds the pupil and controls the amount of light that enters the eye.

↓

Lens

Focuses light onto the retina. **Accommodation** occurs when the curvature of the lens adjusts to alter visual focus — the lens **flattens** for **distant** objects and **fattens** for **close** objects.

↓

Retina

Converts light into impulses that can be transmitted by neurons to the brain.

After light passes through the cornea, pupil, and lens of the eye, it goes through the **vitreous humor** until it reaches the retina. The **retina consists of** several layers of cells, including:

Cones – Photoreceptors that are responsible for color vision and visual acuity. They are concentrated in the central region of the retina, the **fovea.**

Rods – Photoreceptors that are responsible for vision in dim light, peripheral vision, and black-and-white vision. Their density is greatest just outside the fovea, and then gradually decreases toward the periphery of the retina.

Bipolar Cells – Cells through which a visual stimulus passes after going through the rods/cones and before going to the ganglion cells.

Ganglion Cells – The axons of the ganglion cells form the **optic nerve.** The optic nerve carries the visual message to the **occipital lobe** of the brain for interpretation.

Other features of the retina include:

Fovea – Tiny spot in the center of the retina that contains only cones. Visual acuity is greatest at this spot.

Blindspot – Location where optic nerve leaves retina; contains no rods or cones. You cannot see anything that reaches this part of your retina.

Horizontal Cells – Retinal cells that connect rods with other rods and cones with other cones. Appear responsible for **Opponent-Process Theory** of color vision.

Amacrine Cells – Large retinal neurons that connect ganglion cells laterally. The functions of most amacrine cells are unknown. These cells combine messages from adjacent photoreceptors.

Problem Solving Example:

 List the principle parts of the eye and describe their function.

 The human eye is a complex organ consisting of several parts. The cornea is the outer transparent coating in front of the eye. Its function is to protect the internal parts.

The lens is a transparent tissue that focuses the image by changing shape – thickening for near objects and thinning for distant ones. This process is called accommodation, and is carried out by expansion or contraction of the ciliary muscles. Like the cornea, the lens is curved in shape. It bends and focuses light rays onto the retina.

The retina is the photosensitive curtain of nerve cells located at the back of the eye. Over 120 million photoreceptor cells are found in the retina of each eye. There are two types which are named according to their shape: rods and cones. Rods are found throughout the retina area except in the small central region called the fovea. They are highly concentrated along the outer edge of the retina. Rods are extremely sensitive to light energy, most especially to achromatic (black-white) light and dim light; hence, they facilitate night vision.

Cones are located primarily in the fovea. There are about 6 to 7 million cones in each eye. They require large amounts of light energy stimulation before responding. Cones possess the ability to respond differentially to different wavelengths. They are thus sensitive to color (which is dependent on wavelength); it is through the cones that we perceive color.

The pupil is the round opening in the center of the eye through which light passes to the retina. The pupil appears as the black circle in the center of the eye.

The colored portion of the eye is called the iris.

It is the tissue that surrounds the pupil and regulates its size – contracting or dilating in order to adjust the amount of light entering the eye.

3.2.3 Eye to Brain Pathways

The path that visual information travels from the eye to the brain is shown in Figure 3.2. Visual information from the right side of the visual field for each eye exits from the left optic nerve of each eye and meets at the **optic chiasma,** where it is combined and sent to the left side of the brain. Visual information from the left side of the visual field exits from the right optic nerves of both eyes, which also meet at the optic chiasma where they are combined and sent to the right side of the brain. In the brain, the visual information is further processed in the **thalamus** and then sent to the visual cortex located in the **occipital lobe** of each hemisphere. The occipital cortex contains cells known as **feature detectors,** including **simple cells** or **edge detectors** which respond to lines or edges, **complex cells** which respond to the motion and color of objects, and **hypercomplex cells** which respond to an object's orientation, movement, shape, corners, width, color, and length.

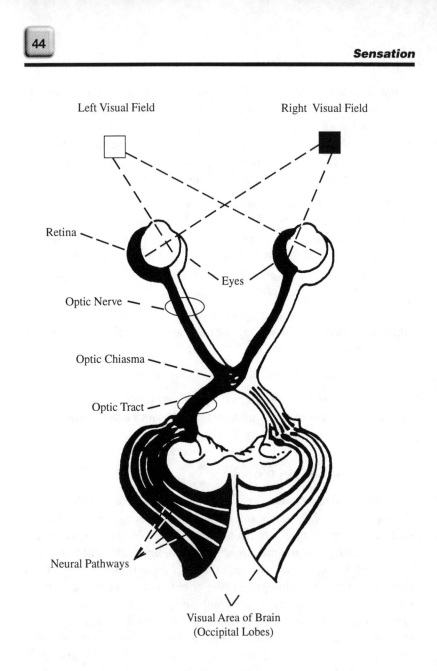

Figure 3.2 Eye to Brain Pathways

Problem Solving Example:

 Trace the path that visual information takes on its way to the brain. Begin with the retinal receptor cells.

 Visual information, first received by the retina's receptor cells, passes through a number of different cells and undergoes a number of transformations before it reaches the brain. First, the information passes through the cell layers of the retina. That is, it is passed through the bipolar and ganglion cell layers. From the ganglion cells, visual information is carried by the optic nerve into the central nervous system.

About half-way to the brain, the optic nerve reaches an intersection called the optic chiasm (from the Greek letter chi, *x*). Here, some fibers from our left eye cross over to proceed to the right side of the brain, and vice versa. Some fibers continue up along the side from which they originate.

Once past the optic chiasm, nerve fibers carrying visual information are called optic tracts. Information from the optic tract is carried to the visual center of the thalamus. This center is called the lateral geniculate body. Finally, the lateral geniculate body relays the information to the visual cortex for final processing.

3.2.4 Light and Dark Adaptation

When entering a darkened room, full **dark adaptation** of the eyes takes place in about 30 to 40 minutes due to a chemical reaction in the rods and cones. The cones adapt first, but they are absolutely **less** sensitive than the rods, so that the absolute threshold for the cones stops decreasing after 10 minutes or so in the dark while the rods continue adapting for 20 or more minutes. The rods cannot discriminate colors, however, and this is why you cannot make out colors in very dim light. When reentering a bright area, the rods quickly lose their dark adaptation and the eyes become **light adapted** as the cones quickly take over.

3.2.5 Color Vision

The three attributes used to describe color are **hue** (determined by wavelength of light; it is the color of visible light), **brightness** (which is a function of the overall intensity of all the wavelengths), and **saturation** (purity or richness of color).

Longer wavelengths of light appear **red** (around 700 nm), **middle wavelengths appear green** (500 nm), and **shorter wavelengths appear blue** (470 nm). **Achromatic colors** cannot be distinguished on the basis of hue. Only **chromatic colors** differ in saturation.

Mixing paints and pigments is **subtractive color mixing** because the two paints being mixed absorb or subtract more wavelengths of light than either one does alone. In subtractive color mixing, yellow mixed with blue results in a green color.

Additive color mixing occurs when beams of light combine. Colored lights **add** their dominant wavelengths to the mixture, stimulating more cones. Both the human eye and color television work according to additive color mixing. Mixing lights produces a color lighter than the darker of the two starting colors. This is why **white** is produced in an additive mixture by mixing all colors together. The **primary colors** of additive mixtures are **red, green, and blue.** These primary colors may be combined in various proportions to match almost all colors. No one primary color can be matched by a mixture of the other two.

For every color, there is another color that is its complement. **Complementary colors** are colors that appear directly opposite one another on the **color circle** and when mixed together in the proper portion, produce a mixture that appears neutral gray. In additive color mixing, yellow and blue are complementary colors and when mixed together, produce gray.

If you stare at a highly saturated patch of color for 20 seconds or so and then look at a white piece of paper, you will see the complementary of the color you were just looking at. When this occurs, it is called a **negative afterimage.**

Problem Solving Example:

 Discuss the three attributes of color. Why do red and pink appear to be different colors?

Our visual system is sensitive to patches of light. We distinguish between different visual impressions generally by three different characteristics: hue, brightness and saturation.

The wavelength of the light determines which "hue" we will perceive. Hue is the generic term that is now applied to what are commonly called colors. Red, orange, yellow, green, blue, indigo, and violet are the basic hues of the spectrum produced by different wavelengths.

When a single wavelength of light is perceived, the hue appears pure or "saturated. " As other wavelengths are added, the hue becomes distilled and appears grayer or less saturated. A mixture of wavelengths in which all the wavelengths were equally strong would appear gray. A deep red is a highly saturated red; whereas a pink is a desaturated red. Saturation produces a "red red" or a "green green."

As the intensity of the light increases the light will appear brighter. Brightness is an aspect of both color (chromatic) and black and white (achromatic) vision. Being hueless, blacks and whites do not differ qualitatively but only in their brightness value. The brightness that we perceive is greatly dependent not only on the energy value of the light intensity but on the state of adaptation of the eye (is the pupil contracted for brightness or enlarged for darkness?) Also brightness varies according to wavelength for a given intensity of light. And conversely, the hue and saturation change somewhat if the brightness is altered.

The **Young-Helmholtz Theory** or **Trichromatic Theory** of color vision proposes that there are three kinds of color receptors in the cones of the eye, one for each of the three primary colors. Physiological data has supported this hypothesis. Three different kinds of cones have been discovered, one sensitive to red light, one sensitive to green light, and one that responds to blue light. According to the Young-Helmholtz

Theory, when you look at a **red object,** the red cones are stimulated to send a message to the brain so that you sense redness. All other colors are perceived as a result of the mixture of red, green, or blue cones being stimulated. A **yellow** object, for example, stimulates green and red cones to respond. The color **white** occurs when red, blue, and green cones are stimulated equally, and **black** results from no cone stimulation.

Hering noted that certain kinds of **color blindness** were not well explained by the Young-Helmholtz Theory. The most common form of color blindness is **red-green blindness.** Individuals with red-green blindness find it difficult to sense red or green but have no trouble seeing yellow. This does not agree with the Young-Helmholtz Theory which implies that yellow is a mixture of red and green. Hering argued that yellow was just as much a primary color as red or green or blue and developed the **Opponent-Process Theory** of color vision.

The Opponent-Process Theory states **red-green receptor,** a **yellow-blue receptor,** and a **dark-light** (or black-white) **receptor.** Only one member of a pair can respond, either red *or* green, yellow *or* blue, dark *or* light, but *not* red *and* green or yellow *and* blue. If one member of a receptor pair is stimulated more than its opponent, the corresponding color will be seen. For example, if red is stimulated more than green, the color red will be seen and vice versa. If both members of a pair are stimulated equally, they cancel each other out and this leaves only gray. (Members from nonopponent pairs may interact and be stimulated at the same time, resulting in colors such as yellow-red or blue-green.)

The **Young-Helmholtz Theory** seems to be a good description of visual processing in the **retina** because cones have been found to be sensitive to red, green, and blue (and not to red-green and blue-yellow). The **Opponent-Process Theory** seems to be a better explanation of color vision at higher levels within the brain – at the **optic nerve and beyond.**

3.3 Hearing

The ear functions to convert sound waves from the external environment into nerve impulses which reach the brain and are then transformed into the sensation we know as sound.

3.3.1 Measuring Sound

Sound travels as a series of **invisible waves** in the air. **Frequency** is one **physical dimension** of sound. The frequency of sound is the number of complete waves that pass a given point in space every second and is measured in units called **hertz (Hz)**. One cycle per second is 1 Hz. The longer the wavelength, the lower the frequency. The human ear can hear between 20 to 20,000 Hz. A **pure tone** is made up of only one frequency. Frequency determines the **pitch** of a sound (how high or low a tone sounds). Pitch is a **psychological dimension** of sound. It varies with frequency but may also be changed by intensity.

Amplitude is another **physical dimension** of sound and refers to the height of the sound waves. It determines the loudness of a sound which is a **psychological dimension**. The loudness of sound is measured in **decibels (dB)**. The **threshold of hearing** is 0 dB. A whisper is about 25 dB, and a normal conversation is 60 dB. A person could experience hearing loss if exposed to sound over 90 dB for a period of time. Sound over about 130 dB can produce pain. The decibel scale is a **logarithmic** one. Thus, a sound that is 100 dB more intense than another sound is 10 million times more powerful.

Problem Solving Example:

What is the relationship between frequency and pitch? What is the relationship between intensity and loudness?

We can distinguish between two tones when they differ with respect to certain variables. One such variable is loudness; one tone may be louder than the other. Another such variable is pitch. Different notes on the piano, for example, may be played equally loud. We would probably still be able to distinguish between them though each note's pitch is different.

Our experiences of pitch and loudness are related to physical aspects of the actual stimulus. For instance, pitch is closely related to the frequency of the stimulus. Sound is basically vibrations of particles in the air. These vibrations are wavelike and are called sound waves. They go up, down, up again, etc. The frequency of a vibration is a measure of how many times it goes up and down in a single period of time, usually a second. If a stimulus goes up and down many times in a second, we say it is a high frequency wave. We generally experience high frequency waves as high-pitched tones. Waves with low frequencies correspond to low-pitched tones.

Similarly, the loudness of a sound is closely related to the intensity of the physical stimulus. Intensity is a measure of the amount of physical energy a stimulus sends to our senses. A high intensity sound sends a great deal of energy to our ear. We experience a high intensity sound as being "loud." Similarly, a low intensity stimulus is perceived as "soft."

However, loudness is not directly related to intensity. Pitch is also not directly related to frequency. Other variables may participate in determining the loudness or pitch of a tone. For example, the intensity of a sound is also important in determining pitch. Increasing the intensity of a sound will often increase its pitch. Frequency may also play a part in determining loudness.

In summary, frequency is very important in determining pitch. Intensity is closely related to experienced loudness. However, other variables are involved in these experiences.

3.3.2. Structure of the Ear

A diagram of the human ear is presented in Figure 3.3.

As sound waves travel through the air in the environment, they funnel into the ear where they collide with the **eardrum** or **tympanic membrane** which is like a tight drumhead within the ear canal. Sound waves set the eardrum in motion which causes three small bones, the **auditory ossicles,** to vibrate by means of a chain reaction. First the

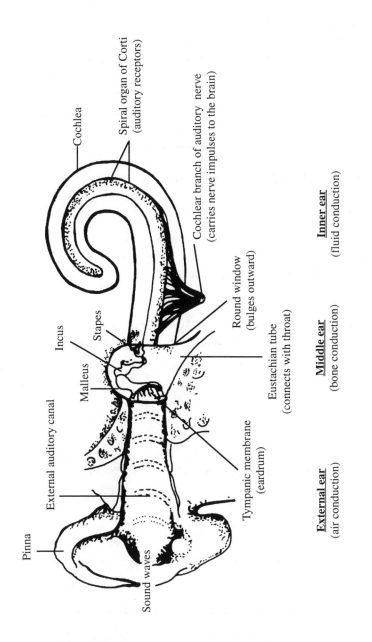

Figure 3.3 Structure of the Auditory System

eardrum causes the **hammer** or **malleus** to vibrate, which in turn sets the **anvil** or **incus** to vibrate, causing the **stirrup** or **stapes** to vibrate. The stirrup is attached to the oval window. As the **oval window** moves back and forth, it sets up waves in the fluid of the **cochlea,** which is a snail-shaped structure that contains the nerve endings essential for hearing. By the time the sound has reached the oval window, it is many times stronger than when it first struck the eardrum. Within the cochlea is the **organ of Corti** which contains about 16,000 hair cells or **cilia.** The movement of the fluid within the cochlea causes the cilia to bend and as they bend, nerve impulses are sent via the auditory nerve, to the brain. The neural pathway from the cochlea to the auditory cortex has been described as the most complicated of all sensory pathways.

The ear can be divided into three sections: the **outer ear,** the **middle ear,** and the **inner ear**. In order to her, the sound wave must enter the outer ear and pass through the middle ear into the inner ear.

Outer Ear

Gathers the sound. Sound travels by means of **air conduction.**
Consists of **pinna (external ear)** and **tympanic membrane**

(eardrum).

↓

Middle Ear

Transmits the sound by means of **bone conduction.** Consists of
malleus (hammer), incus (anvil), and **stapes (stirrup).**

↓

Inner Ear

Transforms sound into **neural energy** by means of **fluid**

conduction. Consists of **oval window, cochlea, cilia,**

basilar membrane, organ of Corti, and

semi-circular canals (determine balance).

Problem Solving Example:

What are the three major parts of the ear? Which important structures does each part contain?

The three major parts of the ear are the outer, middle, and inner ears. The outer ear consists of an ear flap called the pinna, an air-filled tube, and the auditory canal. Sound energy from the environment enters the ear through the pinna and travels down the auditory canal to the middle ear.

The middle ear is separated from the outer ear by a thin membrane which is stretched across the auditory canal. This membrane is called the eardrum. Just behind the eardrum are three small bones, the ossicles of the middle ear. The last of these bones is called the stapes. It lies directly in front of the oval window, a membrane which covers an opening to the inner ear.

The inner ear contains two kinds of sense organs. One is concerned with hearing. The other deals with our sense of balance. The part of the inner ear dealing with hearing is called the cochlea.

The cochlea consists of three fluid filled canals, each separated from the other by a membrane. These canals spiral around inside the cochlea, which is structured much like a snail shell. The cochlea also contains the organ of corti, which has the receptor cells necessary for hearing. In the auditory system, these receptors are small cells with hairs on their ends. These hair cells are located on a membrane called the basilar membrane. Above the hair cells lies the tectorial membrane. In addition, the cochlea contains the round window, another membrane separating the inner and middle ears. It lies below the oval window which was previously discussed.

3.3.3 Theories of Hearing

Several theories have been developed to explain how hearing works. The main question these theories are attempting to answer is how neural impulses are coded within the inner ear to give the brain different kinds of auditory information.

Place theory is based on the idea that different **sound frequencies** actually trigger different neurons along the basilar membrane. The **basilar membrane** is a membrane inside the cochlea that is sensitive to frequency differences in sound vibrations. The **middle frequencies** distort the basilar membrane at the **apex** of the cochlea and **high frequencies** distort the basilar membrane at the **base** of the cochlea, near the oval window. Place theory, therefore, attempts to explain the reception of sound waves between 5,000 and 20,000 Hz by stating that different frequencies stimulate cilia at different places within the cochlea. Place theory has difficulty explaining tones below 5,000 Hz, however. These **low tones** tend to stimulate cilia throughout the **entire organ of Corti.**

Frequency theory accounts for sounds between 20 and 300 Hz, the **lowest tones** heard by the human ear. Frequency theory asserts that neural activity is coded in terms of the **rate**, rather than the place, at which neurons are triggered. Frequency theory is based on the notion that auditory neurons fire at rates correlated with the frequency of the sound. Frequency theory cannot, however, account for high-frequency sounds because it is impossible for a single neuron to fire, recover, and fire again as fast as would be necessary to follow a high frequency tone.

The **volley principle,** an extension of the frequency theory, accounts for tones from 300 to 5,000 Hz (**mid-range frequencies**) in which several neurons fire out of sequence in volleys to sum 300 to 5,000 cycles per second. According to this theory, auditory neurons fire in groups that are correlated with the frequency of the sound.

3.4 The Other Senses

Although vision and hearing are the most studied senses, other senses are important as well.

The four basic **taste** qualities are **sour** (sides of tongue), **sweet** (tip of tongue), **salty** (sides and tip of tongue), and **bitter** (back of tongue).

Taste is a **chemical sense.** The stimuli for taste perception are chemicals absorbed in the saliva that stimulate taste cells located in the **taste buds.** Most of our approximately 10,000 taste buds are located on the tongue, with a few in the throat. They are replaced about every seven days. Preferences for some tastes appear inborn and others appear learned. Newborn infants respond to sweet, sour, salty, and bitter stimuli, although they prefer sweet. The smell, appearance, temperature, etc. of food also affect how its taste is perceived.

Problem Solving Examples:

Q What are three factors that influence the intensity of a taste? Explain.

A We say that some foods taste pleasantly sweet; other foods are too sweet. Thus there are different intensities of sweetness. This applies to other tastes as well. Three major factors influence the intensity of a taste. These are the concentration of the stimulus, the area of the tongue's surface that is stimulated, and other tastes present at the same time.

A glass of salt and water which contains only a pinch of salt will not taste very salty. However, one which contains much salt will taste quite salty. The second glass contains a more 'concentrated' mixture. This means it contains more salt in the same amount of liquid. The salt solutions described show that concentration affects the intensity of a taste. The higher the concentration, generally, the more intense is the taste experienced.

Another variable factor is the amount of tongue that is in contact with the stimulus. This can also affect the intensity of a taste. In general, the larger the area of tongue that is stimulated, the more intense is the taste.

In addition, a process called 'contrast' can affect taste intensity. Two different parts of the tongue may be stimulated by two different tastes at the same time. For example, one can put a weak sugar and water mixture on one side of one's tongue, and a weak salt water mixture on the other. You will find that the salt mixture tastes more intense than it normally would. That is, if the sugar mixture were not there, the salt mixture would not have tasted as salty. We see that we can increase the sensitivity to taste of part of our tongue. This can be done by stimulating another part of our tongue with a different taste. This process is called 'contrast.'

 Certain connoisseurs can recognize hundreds of varieties of wine by tasting small samples. How is this possible when there are only four types of taste receptors?

 Taste buds on the tongue and the soft palate are the organs of taste in human beings. Each taste bud contains supportive cells as well as epithelial cells which function as receptors. These epithelial cells have numerous microvilli that are exposed on the tongue surface. Each receptor is innervated by one or more neurons, and when a receptor is excited, it generates impulses in the neurons. There are four basic taste senses: sweet, sour, bitter, and salty. The receptors for each of these four basic tastes are concentrated in different regions of the tongue-sweet and salty on the front, bitter on the back, and sour on the sides (see Figure). The sensitivity of these four regions on the tongue to the four different tastes can be demonstrated by placing solutions with various tastes on each region. A dry tongue is insensitive to taste.

Few substances stimulate only one of the four kinds of receptors, but most stimulate two or more types in varying degrees. The common taste sensations we experience daily are created by combinations of the four basic tastes in different relative intensities. Moreover, taste does not depend on the perception of the receptors in the taste buds alone. Olfaction plays an important role in the sense of taste. Together they help us distinguish an enormous number of different tastes.

We can now understand how a connoisseur, using a combination of his taste buds and his sense of smell, can recognize hundreds of varieties of wine.

Smell may be one of the oldest senses and is also a **chemical sense.** The receptors for smell are located in the **olfactory epithelium** high up in the roof of the nose. The technical term for smell is **olfaction.** Receptors for smell function in a **lock and key** fashion. Different smells have molecules of certain shapes that fit into receptors that are sensitive to them (like keys fit a certain lock), producing a given odor. **Odorless** substances have a molecular shape that does not stimulate receptors in the olfactory epithelium. Smells that excite sexual interest in animals are called **pheromones.** Olfactory messages are *not* relayed through the thalamus, but pass directly to lower areas of the brain that are **older in evolutionary terms.**

Problem Solving Examples:

 What is the path taken by olfactory information on its way to the brain?

 The olfactory system sends the brain information about odors and fragrances it senses. Actually, what stimulates the sense of smell are small particles called molecules, which enter the nostrils. Once inside, these molecules may touch special long hair cells. These cells translate the physical stimulus of the molecules into electrical information which the brain interprets. These cells relay this information to the brain in the following way.

Olfactory information leaves our nose through bundles of the long hair cells. These bundles travel to a brain center called the olfactory bulb. The olfactory bulb is located at the base of the brain. From here, olfactory information travels directly to the part of the cortex that deals with smell. One of these areas is the olbito frontal cortex, which also processes taste information. This could explain the combining of smell and taste into flavor. Thus we see that this is one of the simplest of our systems. It is difficult to study, though. This is because the cells which are important are practically inaccessible.

 What are three factors that influence our olfactory experience?

 We can easily compile lists of substances which have distinctive smells. For example, many flowers have a specific smell. Also, the odor of garbage is unmistakable. However, we do not yet understand how it is that we can differentiate between these odors. Some factors which are probably involved in 'smell' are: quality, concentration, and rate of flow of the stimulus.

It is thought that every substance has a particular quality which determines its smell. For example, every substance is composed of tiny particles called molecules. The molecules of each substance have a distinctive shape. The shape of the molecules of a substance can be considered a quality of the substance. This quality may be important in determining its smell.

The concentration of a stimulus is also important in determining smell. If ten cans of Lysol were released into one room, the smell would probably be very intense and unpleasant. However, if only a small amount was released, the smell experience would be quite different. The former room was more concentrated with Lysol. This means there was much more Lysol in the same amount of space. So we see that concentration of the stimulus influences olfactory experience.

A third factor involved in 'smell' is the rate of flow of the stimulus. The stimuli for smell are thought to be the gas molecules of the particular substance. Gaseous substances can move or flow. For example, the wind can be thought of simply as flowing air. If the molecules of a stimulus are flowing quickly, the smell will appear strong. If the molecules are not moving that rapidly, the smell will seem weaker.

Thus, the rate of flow of a stimulus also affects our olfactory experience.

Somato senses provide us with information about what is happening on the surface of our bodies and inside our bodies. Imbedded within the skin are many receptors for **touch.** Different touch receptors measure pressure, light touch, vibration, pain, cold, and warmth. Touch receptors are distributed over the body in **receptive fields,** each associated with its own grouping of touch neurons. Touch receptors are unevenly distributed on the skin. For instance, touch receptors are more highly concentrated on the fingertips than on the back. Touch reception is projected to the **somatosensory area** of the **parietal lobes** of the brain. Different locations in the cerebral cortex receive touch information from different parts on the body.

Q What receptors are involved in the four skin senses? What stimulus does each receptor respond to?

A Our skin is sensitive to temperature, vibration, pressure, and pain. These are considered the four skin senses. Psychologists are not certain that specific receptors in the skin correspond to specific skin senses. However, the following distinctions do appear fairly certain.

It seems that free nerve fibers located in the skin are responsible for our temperature sensations. The temperature of our skin is generally slightly lower than that of our blood. Free nerve fibers in the skin respond to changes in the difference between skin and blood temperature. For example, the temperature of our blood is roughly 38°C. The skin temperature of our forearm is usually 33°C. This is a 5° difference. If some ice is put on your arm, the temperature of your skin will be lowered. The difference between your skin and blood temperatures will be increased. This stimulates the free nerves which causes you to feel cold. Investigators have found that cold receptors are close to the skin and warm receptors are located deeper in the tissue.

Pressure, or touch, is another of the skin senses. There are a number of different receptors in the skin that signal that we have been touched. The Meissner corpuscle is one such structure. It is located in the hairless regions of our body. It may be found, for example, in the palms of your hands. The basket nerve ending is located at roots of hairs. It is believed to respond to touch in those body regions that have hair. Finally, small capsules called Pacinian corpuscles are thought to respond when deep pressure is applied to the skin. The Pacinian corpuscles which are visible to the naked eye also detect vibration. Vibrations inform us if a surface is rough or smooth.

The stimulus that the above pressure receptors respond to is the bending or deforming of part of our skin. Therefore, when one first puts a watch on, you feel it. Immediately after, though, you "forget" that it is there. The initial bending of the skin that the watch caused was relayed to your brain by one of the pressure receptors. Therefore, you felt it. However, once the watch is on, your skin remains in the same place. It is no longer being actively bent. The pressure receptors do not respond to this constant pressure. Therefore, you do not feel that you are constantly being 'touched' by your watch.

Pain is the last of the skin senses. It appears that unspecialized free nerve endings in the skin respond to pain. Scientists are not certain exactly what stimulus is needed in order for us to feel pain. There does not seem to be a brain-pain connection. It was first thought that damage to a part of the body causes pain. However, this does not explain how people undergo surgical procedures while under hypnosis. We know that as parts of our body are destroyed, the body repairs them as quickly as it can. It appears, then, that we feel pain when our body is damaged faster than it can be repaired. Pain may also be caused by a chemical released by injured cells. Thus the 'rate' of body damage, rather than the 'amount' of body damage, is thought to be the stimulus for sensations of pain.

The **kinesthetic sense** provides us with information about the position of our body in space. The receptors for the sense of kinesthesis are located in the **joints, tendons,** and **muscles.** Specialized **kinesthetic detectors** in the brain appear to be associated with different postures.

The **vestibular sense** is the sense of **balance.** Its receptors are located in the **semi-circular canals** and **vestibular sacs** located in the **inner ear.** The semi-circular canals are three small, fluid-filled canals located in the inner ear, which contain receptors sensitive to changes in spatial orientation. **Cilia** or **hair cells** in the semi-circular canals are displaced by moving fluid which sends information to the brain about balance and body position. The vestibular sacs are two bag-like structures at the base of the semi-circular canals that also contain receptors for the sense of balance.

What are the vestibular organs, and how do they operate?

Our vestibular organs, located in the inner ear, provide us with a sense of balance. It does this through information about the movements and position of our head. There are two groups of vestibular organs. These are the semicircular canals and the otolith organs.

There are three semicircular canals that respond to changes in the rotation of the head. They are located in the inner part of our ear. Each one lies in a different plane. That is, if they were lying on this paper, one canal would run from top to bottom and another would run across the paper. The third canal would run through the paper and out the back of this book.

The canals are filled with fluid. When our head is rotated, this fluid moves. Which fluid moves depends upon the particular head motion we make. For instance, we can move our head up and down. In this case, the fluid in the canal that is oriented up and down will move. When this fluid moves, it puts pressure on special cells with hairs that are located in the canals. These hair cells send information about our head's movements to the brain.

The canals do not respond to continuous movement. Rather, the hair cells in the canals respond only to changes in the rate of motion of the head. Thus when a dancer is spinning, the semicircular organs are stimulated only when he/she speeds up or slows down.

The otolith organs are small stonelike crystals. They are also located in the inner part of our ear. Unlike the semicircular canals, the otoliths do not respond to movements

Rather, they respond to the actual position of one's head. If your head is upright, gravity stimulates the otolith crystals in a certain way. They then send this information to the brain. The brain interprets this message and concludes that the head is upright.

Together, the semicircular canals and the otolith organs provide one with a sense of balance. You know that you instinctively straighten up when thrown off balance. This could not be done without the information provided by the vestibular organs.

CHAPTER 4

Perception

4.1 Depth Perception

Sensation and perception are related because **perception** involves the **interpretation of sensory information.**

Problem Solving Example:

Differentiate between sensation and perception.

The major senses of the human organism include seeing, hearing, taste, smell, touch (includes warmth, cold, pain, dryness, wetness, etc.), position, motion, and equilibrium. For each sense we have a sense organ that is affected by a particular type of physical energy. The ear, for instance, is responsive to sound waves. Within each sensory realm there are a number of qualities which recur in varying combinations, such as with the sense of hearing – loud, soft, shrill, resonant, humming, screeching, to name just a few of the qualities that can be discerned by the human ear. The different experiences that we are able to discern within each sensory realm are called sensations. The sensations are of a tremendous variety, but can all be reduced to a few basic physical variables. Though the eye can see thousands of different scenes, they are all produced by light; though the ear can hear sounds from a siren to a symphony, they are all produced by differing intensity and frequency vibration of sound waves.

Sensations provide us with basic elementary experiences which we further interpret into meaningful events. This interpretation of sensations is a much more complex process than simply registering and reflecting the external world. It involves encoding, storage (memory), and organization of the sensations that are received. It is this process that is called "perception." A very general characteristic of all perceptual experience is to attend to and organize selectively the data that is provided by the sensory system. Precisely how this is accomplished has intrigued scientists, and their research and experimentation has provided an abundant theoretical basis from which the student can explore the mysteries of how we construct our sense-based reality. The problem of explaining how and why we perceive the way we do is one of the most controversial fields in psychology today.

Nativists and the **direct perception theory** assert that perception is an **innate** mechanism and is a function of **biological organization**. **Empiricists** and the **image and cue theory** believe that perceptions are **learned** based on past experience.

The **ecological view** of perception argues that perception is an automatic process that is a function of information provided by the environment. The **constructionist view** of perception holds that we construct reality by putting together the bits of information provided by our senses.

Perceptual set is a readiness to perceive a stimulus in a particular way.

Depth perception involves the interpretation of **visual cues** in order to determine **how far away** objects are.

There is currently a debate as to whether depth perception is an **inborn ability** or a **learned response** as a result of experience **(nature vs. nurture).**

Gibson and **Walk** (1960) developed an apparatus they called the **visual cliff** that is used to measure depth perception in infants and toddlers. The visual cliff consists of an elevated glass platform divided into two sections. One section has a surface that is textured with a checkerboard pattern of tile, while the other has a clear glass surface with a checkerboard pattern several feet below it so it looks like the floor drops off. Gibson and Walk hypothesized that if infants can perceive depth, they should remain on the "shallow" side of the platform and avoid the "cliff" side, even if coaxed to come across by parents. When they tested infants from 6 to 14 months of age, Gibson and Walk found that infants would crawl or walk to their mothers when the mothers were on the "shallow" side of the platform, but would refuse to cross the "deep" side even with their mothers' encouragements to cross. The results of this and other visual cliff studies still do not prove that depth perception is innate because before infants can be tested, they must be able to crawl and may have already learned to avoid drop-offs.

Two types of visual cues, binocular cues and monocular cues, allow us to perceive depth.

Problem Solving Example:

 Empiricists vs. nativist: discuss these two points of view and give evidence for both sides.

 The nature of perception is still unclear. For many years perception was explained with a structural (the piecing together of different sensations) or empirical (based on experience) theory. The empiricists believed that perception consisted of individual sensations coming together in different combinations with memories of past sensational experiences. This theory assumes that we don't see shapes, distances or forms at all. We see only points of light arranged in various manners. Some of these arrangements have strong nonvisual memories associated with them which give us the ability to measure distance. Thus, the empiricist theory relies a great deal on learning as an explanation for our experience of the world. The perception of, let us say, a blue pillow would then be a learned experience whereby the mass of blue points of light would combine with the memory of past attempts to grasp or move toward a like object giving size and depth cues. Altogether the visual sensations on the retina and the memory of past muscular actions produce the final impression of the blue pillow.

Recent research has uncovered a number of discoveries that have challenged the empiricist position. Infants can, for example, perceive three dimensionality and distance as soon as they are able to locomote, even though we assume that they had no opportunity to learn such perceptual behavior. Also it is difficult to use the empiricist theory for explaining anything more than simple stimuli. More complex stimuli defy the empiricist explanation. For instance, shapes, colors, movements, as soon as they are examined in different contexts are perceived not as the structuralist explanation would expect, (i.e., points of light) but they are greatly influenced by the background on which they are perceived.

These observations tend to support another school of thought on the nature of perception. The "nativists," as the name implies, believe that human perception is innate. They believe that after millions of years of adaptation, the human nervous system is now equipped with connections that make it automatic for an infant to perceive, for example, three-dimensionality. With the state of our knowledge today, it is not possible to determine which of these approaches to perception is most correct. It cannot be clearly demonstrated that perceptual learning occurs early in life and then resists further modification, nor can it be demonstrated that it is innate but subject to modification and new learning. Because of the difficulties involved in examining perceptual processes, especially with infants, it seems that a combination of the two explanations serves us best today.

It is likely that we do have some innate perceptual abilities, and also that they can, to some extent, be modified by experience.

4.1.1　Binocular Cues

Binocular cues for depth require the use of **both eyes.** The two binocular cues are convergence and retinal disparity.

Convergence involves the interpretation of **muscular movements** related to how close or how far away an object is. For an object closer than approximately 25 feet, our eyes must converge (move inward) in order to perceive it as a single object clearly in focus. Our perceptual system uses this muscular movement as a cue for closeness. For an object farther than 25 feet, our eyes tend to focus on infinity (little to no muscular movement required), and again, our perceptual system uses this as a cue that the object must be far away.

Retinal disparity is the difference in locations, on the retinas, of the stimulation by a single object. This means that an object viewed by both eyes will stimulate one spot on the right retina and a different spot on the left retina. This is due to the fact that the object is at a different distance from each eye. Retinal disparity is also used as a cue for depth because the **eyes are set a certain distance apart** in the head, and objects closer than 25 feet are sensed on significantly different locations **on each eye's retina.** Viewing objects that are close causes considerable retinal disparity (very different portions of each retina are stimulated) and viewing objects at a distance creates **little** retinal disparity (similar portions of each retina are stimulated).

4.1.2 Monocular Cues

Monocular cues for depth require the use of **only one eye.** Two-dimensional presentations (e.g., photographs, television) also rely on monocular cues to indicate depth.

Monocular cues for depth include:

Linear Perspective — Parallel lines appear to converge on the horizon (e.g., railroad tracks).

Relative Size — Closer objects appear larger; the larger of two figures will always appear closer because the two objects will project retinal images of different sizes.

Overlap or Interposition — Objects that are overlapped or partially concealed by other objects will appear farther away.

Gradient of Texture — Objects that are closer have greater detail or texture than those far away.

Aerial Perspective — Close objects are bright and sharp; distant objects are pastel and hazy.

Relative Motion or Motion Parallax — When moving our head from side to side, nearby objects appear to move more than distant objects; far objects appear to move slower than nearby objects.

Height on a Plane or Height in a Field — Objects that are closer appear to be lower in the field than objects that are farther away.

Looming Effect or Optical Expansion — When we approach objects, objects close to us appear to be moving toward us faster than those farther away.

Accommodation — Lens of eye must bend or adjust to bring to focus objects that are relatively close (see Chapter 3).

4.2 Perceptual Organization

We tend to **organize** our sensations into meaningful perceptions.

Perceptual organization is the basis of **Gestalt psychology.** Gestalt psychologists assert that we tend to organize our perceptions immediately into **wholes,** and emphasize that the whole is **greater than** the sum of its parts.

Gestaltists have presented a number of descriptive principles of perceptual organization:

Figure-ground — We group some sensations into an object or "figure" that stands out on a plain background. The figure is the distinct shape with clearly defined edges and the ground has no defined edges. **Reversible** or **ambiguous figures** have no clearly defined figures and backgrounds (the figure and background can be reversed).

Similarity — Stimuli that are similar in size, shape, color, or form tend to be grouped together.

Nearness or Proximity — Stimuli that are near each other tend to be grouped together.

Continuity — Perceptions tend toward simplicity or continuity; lines tend to be seen as following the smoothest path; lines

Delboeuf

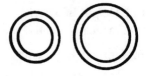

Judd

Müller - Lyer

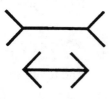

Ponzo

Ebbinghaus

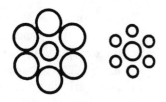

Figure 4.1 Visual Illusions

interrupted by an overlapping object are seen as belonging together if they result in straight or gently curving lines when connected.

Closure — Figures that have gaps in them are seen as completed and are perceived as recognizable figures.

Common Fate — Objects that move together tend to be grouped together.

Simplicity — Every stimulus pattern is perceived in such a way that the resulting structure is as simple as possible.

Orientation — Objects with the same orientation are seen as part of a group.

Apparent Motion or Phi Phenomenon — Perceived motion when the object is, in fact, stationery. (For example, when two lights are placed side by side in a darkened room and flashed alternately, one light moving back and forth is perceived.)

Problem Solving Example:

Q Discuss Gestalt's Laws of Organization.

A Gestalt theory followed structuralism as a leading explanation of the human perceptual system. The Gestalt theorists rejected the structural idea that our perceptions were based on an assemblage of separate points of sensation and concerned themselves more with larger units of perception: the forms, figures and the contexts within which they were set. This concentration on the perception of form led to the systematic study of the stimulus determinants of shape and form. From this study emerged a group of "laws" of organization. It is questionable whether they rightly deserve the title "laws" as they are mainly theoretical constructs that yet require further investigation to determine their correctness as explanations of perceptual processes.

There are numerous organizational laws. Five of the most important ones are:

1. Area: The smaller a closed portion of a representation, the more it is likely to look like a figure. The larger the enclosed area, the less likely the eye is to organize it as a whole.

2. Closedness: Areas that are closed are more likely to be seen as figures than are those portions of a representation that have open contours.

3. Proximity: Items that are placed close together are likely to be grouped together in a logical manner. Long horizontal rows of dots are likely to be organized as horizontal lines rather than vertical lines until the vertical line becomes longer than the horizontal, at which point they will be viewed as vertical lines.

4. Continuation: An arrangement that makes the fewest interruptions in a curving or a straight line will be organized as a figure.

5. Symmetry: The more symmetrical a closed area is the more likely it is to be seen as a figure.

These laws have a principle in common which has been called the Minimum Principle. That is, the eye tends to see that which is simplest to see.

Though the principles behind the Gestalt approach to perception are today in question, the contribution of this line of research to the description of the cues which determine which part of the visual field belongs to the same object or form has been invaluable.

4.3 Perceptual Constancies

Another important characteristic of visual perception is the **perceptual constancy** or **stability** of the shape, size, brightness, and color of objects in our visual fields. We are able to recognize the same objects at a variety of angles, at various distances, and even under different colored lighting because of perceptual constancies:

Size Constancy — Objects we are familiar with are perceived as their true size despite changes in the distance between us and the objects.

Shape Constancy — Objects appear to be the same shape despite changes in their orientation toward the viewer.

Brightness or Lightness Constancy — Objects appear to stay the same brightness despite changes in the amount of light falling on them.

Color Constancy — The hue of an object appears to stay the same despite changes in background lighting.

Problem Solving Examples:

Why is an array of equally spaced dots perceived as rows and columns?

The Gestalt theorists have compiled a long list of variables that influence our perception of form and shape. One of the overriding factors affecting the way in which we organize an impression is simplicity. We tend to organize ambiguous representations into the most simple pattern available. There are a number of factors that appear to contribute to simplicity which were pointed out by the Gestaltists in the form of "laws" of organization. Though it has been difficult to objectively demonstrate that these "laws" of organization do contribute to simplicity, recent research has begun to make it possible to develop objective standards for recognizing simplicity.

One of the major components of simplicity is proximity. Dots or objects that are placed closely together tend to be grouped together in some kind of meaningful configuration. Columns and rows are organized figures that the eye sees easily and it tends to organize unconnected, yet closely placed objects into a familiar pattern. Whether this tendency to simplicity is inborn or learned, we don't know. We do know, however, that the nervous system seems to choose to see the world in the most simple and constant way possible.

If asked how tall a person across the street is, you can give an accurate estimation. Discuss this perceptual phenomenon.

A Our perceptual system relishes simplicity and constancy. Although, as the distance between the eye and an object increases, the image on the retina undergoes great size changes, we do not perceive this change, and tend to see the object as the same size. We also tend to see large objects as large and small objects as small no matter what their actual apparent size to the eye. A distant mountain may appear on the retinal screen smaller than the tree we are standing next to, but we will still perceive the mountain as larger than the tree.

We are also capable of taking distance into account when we are judging size. Though this calculation occurs automatically, it is usually quite accurate. It is this capacity to judge the size of an object by the combined information from the retinal image and the compensation for apparent distance that makes it possible to look across the street and correctly estimate the height of a person.

Another phenomenon that probably contributes to this ability to estimate size of a person at a distance is "familiar size." This is a traditional depth cue. That is, our familiarity with the usual size of a person helps us to know the approximate distance they are from us. If the person across the street were a child, we would automatically calculate the probable height of the child using our knowledge of the usual size of a child.

4.4 Perceptual Illusions

An **illusion** is an **incorrect** or **inaccurate perception** of the stimulus being presented. An illusion is *not* the same as an **hallucination** where there is *no* stimulus being perceived.

There is evidence that **learning** might have an important bearing on the perception of illusions. There are individual differences in how (and how strongly) illusions are perceived, and illusions tend to diminish in effect the more you observe them.

Psychologists study illusions because they help us understand underlying perceptual processes. Illusions occur because of cues in the environment. Motivation, expectancy, and/or experiences "trick" us into perceiving things incorrectly.

Some common visual illusions are presented in Figure 4.1. These and other illusions are described below.

In the **Ponzo illusion,** the top horizontal line appears to be longer when, in fact, it is identical in length to the bottom line. Because the top line appears farther away, the principle of **size constancy** as well as the **size distance hypothesis** help explain this illusion. The size distance hypothesis is based on size constancy and states that if two objects project the same retinal image but appear at different distances from the viewer, the object that appears farther away from the viewer will typically be perceived as larger. Because the top line in the Ponzo illusion looks farther away (because of linear perspective) than the bottom line, we perceive the distant line to be longer.

The center horizontal lines in both figures of the **Müller-Lyer illusion** are the same length, but the one in the top figure is perceived as longer. This is because the apparent length of both straight lines is distorted by the arrowheads added to the ends. The same is true for the **Judd illusion** where the line segments on either side of the center dot are actually equal in length.

The **Ebbinghaus illusion** occurs because of **comparative size.** The center circle of the figure on the left looks smaller than the corresponding center circle of the figure on the right even though they are both the same size. The center circles are perceived incorrectly because of the comparisons made relative to their surrounding circles. The same is true for the **Delboeuf illusion** where the outer circle of the left figure is actually identical to the inner circle of the figure on the right.

The **moon illusion** refers to the phenomenon of the moon appearing larger when it is viewed at the horizon than at the zenith, even though both retinal images are identical. The moon illusion can be explained by the **size distance hypothesis.** Because the apparent shape of the sky is flattened when viewing a moon at the horizon, this may make the moon appear farther away and thus larger.

Problem Solving Example:

 Why does line A seem longer than line B even though they are the same length?

The figures represented by A and B are classic Müller-Lyer patterns. They are an example of a perceptual illusion. The two lines are of the same length though B appears to be shorter than A. The pervasiveness and strength of illusions such as this one has contributed to the great amount of interest in them and investigation of their possible causes. The only way that most illusions or perceptual errors can be detected is by taking an actual physical measuring instrument, like a ruler, and measuring them. Thus far, no reliable means of predicting the effects of illusions or even of anticipating their occurrence has been found, though a number of theories have been set forth.

One theory that has attempted to explain the Müller-Lyer illusion is known as the perspective theory of illusions. According to this theory, the converging lines in line B suggest the depth cue of linear perspective which makes that line appear to be nearer to the viewer than line A. This explains the illusion as being due to the unconscious action of a depth cue.

The apparent sizes of the two lines are the same on the retinal image but because of the perspective depth cue, the mind corrects for distance and B looks shorter than A.

Quiz: Sensation — Perception

1. The transparent outer bulge in front of the eye is the

    (A) lens.

    (B) periphery.

    (C) fovea.

    (D) cornea.

2. Dark adaptation

    (A) increases brightness sensitivity.

    (B) occurs, paradoxically, in the light.

    (C) develops color perception.

    (D) raises the visual threshold.

3. The sensitivity of the eye to light varies with

    (A) wavelength.

    (B) the eye's state of adaptation

    (C) the region of the retina stimulated.

    (D) All of the above.

4. Skin mapping shows that spots of greatest sensitivity for heat and cold are in

    (A) different places.

    (B) the same place.

    (C) alternating locations.

    (D) equidistant from each other.

5. What theory attempts to explain the reception of sound waves between 5,000 and 20,000 Hz?

    (A) Volley theory

    (B) Frequency theory

    (C) Place theory

    (D) None of the above.

6. The vestibular sense is the sense of

    (A) taste.

    (B) balance.

    (C) touch.

    (D) smell.

7. _____ assert(s) that perception is an innate mechanism and is a function of biological organization.

    (A) Nativists

    (B) Direct perception theory

    (C) Both A and B

    (D) Neither A or B

8. The moon illusion refers to the phenomenon of the moon appearing _____ when it is viewed at the horizon than at the zenith even though both retinal images are _____ .

    (A) smaller; larger

    (B) larger; smaller

    (C) smaller; identical

    (D) larger; identical

9. The threshold of hearing is

    (A) 0 dB.

    (B) 25 dB.

    (C) 90 dB.

    (D) 130 dB.

10. The Young-Helmholtz Theory of color vision proposes that there are _____ kinds of color receptors in the cones of the eye.

    (A) one

    (B) two

    (C) three

    (D) four

ANSWER KEY

1. (D)   6. (B)

2. (A)   7. (C)

3. (D)   8. (D)

4. (A)   9. (A)

5. (C)   10. (C)

CHAPTER 5

States of Consciousness

5.1 Sleeping and Consciousness

Consciousness includes not only our awareness of stimuli in the external environment but also our recognition of internal events, such as what we are thinking, an increased heart rate, pain, etc. Consciousness is, therefore, our continually changing stream of mental activity.

The **active mode** of consciousness involves **controlled** or **heightened awareness** and involves planning, making decisions, and responding to those decisions. The **passive mode** of consciousness relates to **minimal awareness** and includes daydreaming and sleeping.

Altered states of consciousness occur any time the content or quality of conscious experience undergoes a significant change. Most research on altered states of consciousness has focused on sleep, dreams, hypnosis, meditation, and the use of psychoactive substances or drugs.

Sleep is defined as a state of consciousness in which the body engages in some housekeeping tasks such as digestion and waste product removal.

Problem Solving Example:

 What is meant by the term consciousness?

A To the average person, consciousness refers to wakefulness or alertness. An individual who is conscious is awake and aware of himself and his surroundings. An unconscious person is not aware of anything. In psychology, however, consciousness does not merely refer to an all-or-nothing state of wakefulness. Consciousness refers to the sum total of mental experiences.

Consciousness exists at different levels in a wide range of graded states. These mental experiences include: coma (which results from severe physical injury), dreaming, fatigue or dullness, wakefulness, alertness, full activity and creative thinking, and hyperactivity. Man experiences all but the most extreme of these states in everyday life.

Each state of consciousness contains varying levels of activity. An individual is least active if he is in a coma state of consciousness and most active in a hyperactive state. During waking states, man engages in a wide variety of activities: thinking, talking, looking, listening. Several of these activities may be performed simultaneously. One of the most prominent activities man engages in is talking to himself, carrying out a constant monologue which many equate with thinking.

Davis (1962) established three criteria an individual must meet to be considered conscious. The person must be aware of:

1. self – he must be able to recognize himself as distinguished from the environment;

2. time – he must be able to discriminate between the presentation in the external world.

3. location in space – he must have a sense of his location in the external world.

5.1.1 Circadian Rhythms

Circadian rhythm or biological clock refers to a person's daily sleep and wakefulness cycle that appears to be controlled, at least in part, in an area of the **hypothalamus** called the **suprachiasmatic nucleus.**

External cues can also influence circadian rhythms. Such cues include the light and dark of day and night.

The high point of wakefulness is related to **increased** body temperature and cortisol levels with vision, hearing, smell, taste, and alertness at their peak.

The low point of wakefulness is related to **decreased** body temperature and cortisol levels and increased sleepiness.

The tendency to adopt a **25-hour cycle** (instead of 24-hour) and as a result go to sleep later and later on succeeding nights is known as **free-running.** This tends to happen when there are no time cues available.

Jet lag occurs when there is a discrepancy between our biological clock and the official clock. Traveling across time zones creates this discrepancy and can result in fitful sleep and a sluggish feeling.

5.1.2 Sleep Patterns

All animals seem to need sleep but in varying amounts. For example, a cat sleeps, on average, 14 hours per day. An elephant sleeps only 2 to 4 hours per day. The average adult human sleeps around 7 to 8 hours. Human infants spend around 16 hours per day sleeping, though this amount decreases as they get older. After the age of 70, the average person sleeps about 6 hours per day. **Healthy insomniacs** can get by on as little as 3 hours of sleep per day.

Researchers have not found many systematic differences between those who habitually sleep more or less each day.

5.1.3 Stages of Sleep

The same stages of sleep appear in all mammals, although the pattern may vary.

Our brain waves, as measured by **EEG patterns,** vary depending on our state of consciousness. For instance, **EEG beta waves** are associated with being awake. Generally, as we move from an awake state through deeper stages of sleep, our brain waves **decrease in frequency** (cycles per second) and **increase in amplitude** (height).

Researchers have found that when we sleep, we cycle through a series of five distinct states:

Alpha Waves – Drowsy but awake state when the eyes are closed and relaxed.

Stage 1 Sleep – Transition between wakefulness and real sleep. **Theta waves.** EEG pattern changes to small, irregular pattern. After 5-10 minutes, move on to Stage 2. Wake up in this stage of sleep.

Stage 2 Sleep – Sleep **spindles** occur. Muscles less tense, eyes rest. EEG during this stage generally irregular, containing theta activity, sleep spindles and K complexes. After 15 minutes, go on to Stage 3. Half of our sleep time is in Stage 2.

Stage 3 Sleep – EEG **delta waves** appear about 20-50 percent of time. Slow-wave sleep.

Stage 4 Sleep – Over half the waves are **delta.** Most difficult to awaken from; deepest sleep. Decreases with age.

We spend the first 30 to 45 minutes going from Stage 1 to Stage 4 sleep. The next 30 to 45 minutes is spent reversing the direction, from Stage 4 back to Stage 1. At this point, **REM sleep** occurs.

REM or **rapid eye movement** sleep is sometimes referred to as **paradoxical sleep** or **active sleep** because although individuals are asleep, their EEG patterns resemble those of someone who is active and awake. Heart rate, respiration, blood pressure, and other physiological patterns are like those occurring during the day. There is also a loss of muscle tone or paralysis called **atonia** during REM sleep. Most of our **dreaming** also occurs during REM sleep. Atonia during REM sleep may keep sleepers from acting out their dreams.

Sleepers are hard to awaken from REM sleep and will often incorporate an unexpected sound from their environment (e.g., alarm clock) into their dreams. By incorporating environmental stimuli, the brain may be avoiding REM sleep disruption.

When deprived of REM sleep, **REM rebound** can occur whereby the sleeper will drop into REM sleep very soon after falling asleep on subsequent nights and will engage in more REM sleep than usual.

Non-REM sleep (NREM) does not include rapid eye movements and is sometimes referred to as **orthodox sleep.** NREM sleep consists of sleeping hours when REM sleep is not occurring and few dreams occur. Sleeptalking and sleepwalking occur during NREM sleep.

During the night, we travel back and forth through the stages of sleep four to six times. Each completed cycle takes about 90 minutes. During the first half of the night, most of the time is spent in deeper sleep and only a few minutes in REM. The last half of the night is dominated by Stage 2 and REM sleep, from which we wake up.

Both the total amount of sleep per night and the proportion of REM sleep change with age. We tend to sleep less as we get older and the total amount of REM sleep decreases. Infants spend about eight hours per day in REM sleep; adults spend about one to two hours per day in REM sleep.

Problem Solving Example:

 Identify and describe the four stages of sleep. Define and describe Stage 1-REM.

Only recently scientists have been able to analyze sleep. This was made possible by the invention of the electroencephalograph (EEG) – a machine that can measure and record brain waves – the brain's recurrent electrical patterns. The changes that these patterns undergo during sleep are recorded by the EEG for researchers to analyze. Based on such changes, scientists have divided sleep into four stages.

Before actual sleep, a subject is in a relaxed waking state with his eyes closed. The EEG illustrates this state in the form of alpha brain waves or alpha rhythm, a wave pattern of 10 cycles per second. Sleep begins with the onset of Initial Stage 1 EEG. Here, the alpha rhythm is replaced by slower, irregular waves. However, this EEG pattern is not very different from that found in an active, awake person. As the individual falls further into sleep, the wave pattern increases to 14 cycles per second bringing the person into Stage 2 sleep. This stage is characterized by spindles – sharply pointed waves recorded by the EEG. Larger and slower delta waves appear in Stage 3 of sleep. These waves measure one to two cycles per second. Both spindles and delta waves appear in Stage 3. However, in Stage 4, delta waves predominate. The entire cycle of Stages 1 through 4 is executed four to six times during an average eight-hour period of sleep.

Another important stage of sleep is called Stage 1–REM. Eugene Aserinsky found that rapid eye movements (REMs) occur during Stage 1 EEG. These REMs are jerky movements of the eyes beneath the eyelids. REMs are detected and measured by a machine called an electroculogram (EOG). In his research, Aserinsky found that in about 80 percent of the time, subjects who were awakened during these periods reported a dream.

Dreams generally occur during this stage, although dreamlike activity can occur in other stages of sleep. The Stage 1-REM is a period of deep sleep even though its EEG pattern is similar to that of an active, awake individual. For this reason, it has been called "paradoxical sleep."

As each cycle of sleep is repeated, the Stage 1-REM becomes longer. The first one occurs about 90 minutes after sleep has begun and lasts for about 5 to 10 minutes. The stage increases in duration at each 90 minute cycle. As expected, the last Stage 1-REM stage is the longest. During this stage, the sleeper experiences the longest and most vivid dreams. A dream during this stage can last from half an hour to an hour. This last dream is the one that is most likely to be recalled. Quite often, the individual awakens during the last Stage 1-REM.

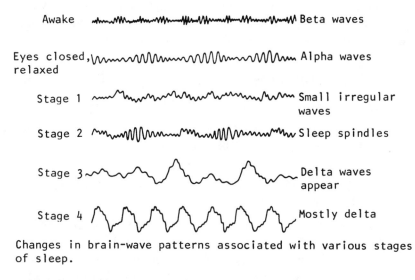

Awake — Beta waves

Eyes closed, relaxed — Alpha waves

Stage 1 — Small irregular waves

Stage 2 — Sleep spindles

Stage 3 — Delta waves appear

Stage 4 — Mostly delta

Changes in brain-wave patterns associated with various stages of sleep.

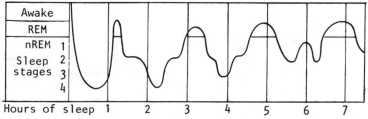

Typical Changes in Stages of Sleep During the Night

5.1.4 Theories of Sleep

Several theories attempt to answer the question of why we need to sleep.

The **adaptive theory** states that each species needs a certain amount of time awake in order to survive and that sleep is an adaptive mechanism that protects members of a species by keeping them out of trouble during time not devoted to survival activities (e.g., eating).

The **conserving energy theory** argues that sleep is a protective method for conserving energy because we burn fewer calories while sleeping.

The **restorative function theory** states that sleep is necessary for resting and restoring the body, for nervous system development, and for consolidating what has been learned during the day.

5.1.5 Sleep Disorders

Sleep disorders trouble many people. Sleep disorders include:

Insomnia – Either have difficulty *falling* asleep or problems *staying* asleep. Causes include depression, drugs or alcohol, irregular circadian rhythm (e.g., jet lag), or stress. Treatments include psychotherapy, medication, and going to bed and arising at the same time each day.

Narcolepsy – Uncontrollable, recurring, sudden onset of REM sleep. Total loss of muscle control. Most likely precipitated by strong emotion, sudden physical effort, or stress. Exact cause unknown. Associated with disturbances in brain stem. Medication is usual treatment.

Sleep Apnea – Frequent stoppages of breathing during sleep that last at least 20 seconds. Sleep is interrupted to restore breathing. Can result in heavy snoring, snorting, and daytime sleepiness. Rarely realize breathing has stopped.

Night Terror – Sudden awakening in which sleeper may sit up, eyes open with a look of terror, and may scream. Occurs during NREM sleep. Usually not remembered in morning.

Hypersomnia – Excessive sleep; more than 12 hours daily. Difficulty awakening and drowsiness throughout day. Causes include severe depression, drug dependence, and physical disorders.

Sleepwalking or Somnambulism – Walking or sitting up in bed during NREM sleep. Eyes may be open but are unseeing. Sleepwalker lacks critical judgment.

Sleeptalking – Talking during NREM sleep. Speech usually not understandable. More common in children.

Nightmares – Disturbing dreams that occur during REM sleep.

Problem Solving Example:

 Discuss the incidence of somnambulism. What explanations have been offered for it?

Somnambulism, or sleepwalking as it is more commonly called, is reported to exist in 1 to 5 percent of the population. The incidence has been found to be high among males, children, and among those who have suffered from enuresis (bedwetting) and have had a family history of somnambulism.

Psychology offers several explanations for somnambulism. Some psychologists regard it as a dissociative state in which there is a loss of memory and awareness of identity. Others regard it as a dreamlike disturbance of consciousness. Because sleepwalking is more common in children than adults, it is often viewed as an immature habit pattern. If sleepwalking persists into adulthood, a more severe diagnosis is applied.

Some researchers consider somnambulism as a symptom of an epileptic state. They have found that a higher frequency of EEG abnormalities occurs among sleepwalkers than non-sleepwalkers. Sleepwalking usually begins in delta sleep.

Psychologists share very different views on the actual condition of sleepwalking. Some psychologists report that it is a state in which the individual is not awake. Others describe it as a state in which the person is not asleep. Psychologists generally disagree about motor ability during this state. Psychologists generally agree that after he awakens, the sleepwalker experiences total amnesia for the somnambulistic incident. A single sleepwalking episode usually lasts approximately 15 to 30 minutes.

5.2   Dreaming

Dreaming is a mental experience that occurs during sleep and consists of vivid images. While we dream, we accept bizarre happenings without question. Most dreaming occurs during REM sleep. **Lucid dreaming** occurs when a sleeper is aware of dreaming while a dream is happening.

There are different theories concerning what dreams are:

Psychoanalytic Theory – Dreams are repressed desires and provide access to the unconscious in symbolic form. Sexual and aggressive impulses are disguised in our dreams.

Activation-Synthesis Model – Dreaming is the brain's attempt to make sense out of random electrical activity that enters the forebrain during REM sleep. Dreams are a response to this random electrical activity and have no meaning.

Housekeeping Hypothesis – The cleaning up or clearing out of unneeded neural connections occurs during dreaming, which is why the brain creates the random electrical activity.

Off-Line Hypothesis – REM sleep plays a role in learning by integrating new and old information.

Problem Solving Example:

 Discuss the effects of REM deprivation during sleep.

 Dreaming occurs during the Stage 1-REM period of sleep. Aserinsky and Kleitman (1953) reported incidents of increased heart rate and breathing during these periods of rapid eye movements. Other researchers have reported that the body's central nervous system is active during this period, undergoing severe fluctuations in heartbeat and blood pressure.

Studies have been conducted on REM deprivation in which subjects slept but were awakened each time they entered the REM period. A control group was also employed whose subjects were awakened the same number of times as the REM-deprived subjects, but only during non-REM periods. Researchers found that during each successive night of the experiment, the REM-deprived subjects entered into more REM periods. During the day, these subjects appeared more tense, irritable and generally more anxious than the control group subjects. The REM-deprived subjects experienced difficulty in concentrating and remembering. When the experimenters finally allowed the REM-deprived subjects to sleep without interruption, the sleepers dreamed 60 percent more than usual.

This additional dreaming has been called "REM rebound." These studies seem to indicate that man has a need to dream.

5.3 Hypnosis

Hypnosis comes from the Greek word **Hypnos,** the Greek god of sleep. Hypnotized people, however, are not asleep.

Franz Anton Mesmer (1734-1815), an Austrian physician, popularized **mesmerism** (now called hypnosis) in order to cure patients.

Hypnosis is a systematic procedure used to produce a heightened state of suggestibility. Hypnosis can lead to enhanced fantasy and role-taking abilities, reduced reality testing and planfulness, and redistributed attention.

Posthypnotic suggestions are suggestions made during hypnosis that influence a person's later behavior. **Posthypnotic amnesia** occurs when hypnotized subjects are told they will remember nothing that happened while they were hypnotized.

Age regression is a term that describes hypnotized subjects who are behaving as if they are reliving experiences from childhood.

Dissociation involves the splitting off of mental processes into two or more separate, simultaneous streams of awareness. Hypnotized subjects can then perform acts that do not register in their conscious memory or can engage in two behaviors while remembering only one of them. **Automatic writing** is an example of dissociation and occurs when a hypnotized subject writes something without being aware of it and while discussing something else.

Dissociation Theory states that hypnosis is a splitting of central control of thought processes and behavior. The hypnotized subject agrees to give some control to the hypnotist.

According to **role theory,** people play the role of being hypnotized and thus comply with the hypnotist's directions.

State theory says that hypnosis is a special state of consciousness and that significant changes in basic mental processes take place during hypnosis.

Self-hypnosis occurs without the aid of a hypnotist. **Highway hypnosis** is a form of self-hypnosis that can occur while driving a car. People can drive great distance with no conscious memory of responding to traffic signals, other cars, etc.

Not everyone can be hypnotized. Special tests, such as the **Hypnotic Susceptibility Scale,** can measure how **susceptible** one is to hypnosis. Individuals most susceptible to hypnosis tend to have active imaginations, good concentrative ability, proneness to fantasy, and think favorably about hypnosis. **Willingness** to be hypnotized is also an important factor.

Hypnosis is used as a substitute for **anesthetic drugs** and to help control pain by some patients.

Hypnosis cannot directly improve memory; it can be used, however, to reduce anxiety that may inhibit remembering.

Problem Solving Examples:

 Define hypnosis. How is it induced? Describe neutral hypnosis.

 Hypnosis is defined as a state of consciousness in which the subject experiences a relaxed mental state that lacks the ongoing thought processes which ordinarily occur in normal consciousness. Hypnosis is not a form of sleep. The EEG seen in hypnosis is similar to that of the waking, active state. A subject under hypnosis is completely relaxed, operates his mind and body involuntarily, and is in a state of hypersuggestibility: he readily accepts suggestions from the hypnotist.

Hypnosis is induced while the subject is either sitting or lying down. The hypnotist usually asks the subject to relax and free himself from any stress or anxiety. The hypnotist will suggest to the subject that he is becoming sleepy in order to make him thoroughly relaxed (but not necessarily asleep). The hypnotist builds on those suggestions to which the subject responds early in the session in order to assure the subject that he moves into a deeper hypnotic state. Sometimes, the hypnotist uses a gadget during the induction procedure. This apparatus has no purpose other than to make the hypnotist appear more "scientific" in the subject's eyes, thereby increasing the subject's confidence in him.

In neutral hypnosis the subject is completely relaxed and detached, although still attentive to the hypnotist's suggestions. No suggestions are made about any specific future event. This state arises after the hypnotist's long and repetitious suggestions about sleep and relaxation. Subjects in this state usually describe their minds as being a blank.

 Discuss some applications of hypnosis.

Hypnosis is an important experimental tool in psychology. In addition, it serves important medical and psychiatric purposes in such areas as dentistry, obstetrics and psychotherapy. Hypnosis has been applied to almost every branch of medicine.

Hypnosis has been extremely useful as a pain-killer in the treatment of cancer patients. Hypnosis has been found to reduce pain to such a high degree that morphine becomes superfluous. Decades ago, before chemical anesthetics were available, hypnosis was used widely as an analgesic in surgery. Hypnosis is used to relieve stress in a wide variety of situations and to overcome undesirable habits such as smoking and overeating.

Hypnosis has been found to have a high entertainment value. In this area it has often been used in an unethical manner. People enjoy seeing others behave in bizarre ways. Due to these public displays, many have regarded it as a form of magic and as a result, hypnotism has attracted much skepticism. Despite this, scientific experiments have shown that hypnosis is an altered state of consciousness.

5.4   Meditation

Meditation includes a group of techniques that attempt to focus attention and promote relaxation. It involves a deliberate attempt to alter consciousness.

Concentrative meditation involves focusing all attention on one thing – one word, one item, one sound, etc. – while sitting back and breathing deeply. This results in the same information being cycled through the nervous system repeatedly. The goal is to become nonresponsive to the external environment.

Early researchers reported that meditation produces decreased heart rate, blood pressure and oxygen consumption as well as increased body temperature at the extremities and muscle relaxation. EEG **alpha waves** become more prominent. Later researchers concluded that meditation is no more effective than other relaxation techniques.

Problem Solving Example:

 Define meditation. What are its general purposes?

 Meditation is an altered state of consciousness. Through physical and mental exercises the subject achieves a state of relaxation and tranquility which allows him to gain insight into himself and to discover the meaning of worldly objects. Meditation requires an intense and concentrated effort to rid the mind of daily concerns and thoughts so that a state of mystical union or transcendence may be achieved.

Meditation is typically associated with Eastern religions. But Western religions, particularly Roman Catholicism, have also employed its practice. The two most popular types of meditation are Yoga (from the Hindu tradition) and Zen (from the Buddhist tradition).

The foremost purpose of meditation is the attainment of truth and permanent happiness. Those who engage in meditation believe that because people are basically hedonistic – always behaving in such a way so as to attain pleasure and avoid pain – their range of perceptions is narrow. Thus, people don't see reality as a whole and don't recognize the truth; they live in a world of illusion. As these illusions build, one becomes severed from himself and the outside world. As a result, one never achieves eternal happiness. Meditation techniques are designed to cut through illusions so that the individual may perceive truth directly.

The following is a function definition of the term:

Meditation is a nonintellectual process that removes a person's illusions so that he may reach a state of consciousness from which he can clearly perceive truth.

5.5 Drugs

Drugs are also used in deliberate attempts to alter one's state of consciousness. The drugs that people use **recreationally** are psychoactive. **Psychoactive drugs** are chemical substances that influence the brain, alter consciousness, and produce psychological changes.

Drug abuse or **recreational drug use** is the self-administration of drugs in ways that deviate from either the medical or social norms of a society. **Addiction** is a **physical dependence** in which continued use of a psychoactive drug is necessary to prevent withdrawal symptoms. **Withdrawal symptoms** vary with different drugs, but may include nausea, headache, chills, and craving for the drug. **Avoiding** these withdrawal symptoms **motivates** a person who is addicted to continue using the drug. **Tolerance** refers to a progressive decrease in a person's responsiveness to a drug and as a result, increasing amounts of the drug are required to produce the same effect. Most drugs produce tolerance effects, but they vary in how rapidly they occur.

Psychological dependence can occur without addiction and exists when one must continue to take a drug in order to satisfy mental and emotional cravings for the drug. The psychological pleasure received from using the drug is what **motivates** a person who is psychologically dependent.

Several **major categories** of psychoactive drugs, including depressants, stimulants, hallucinogens, and narcotics, are discussed in the next sections.

5.5.1 Depressants

Depressants or sedatives are drugs that depress the functioning of the central nervous system.

Examples:

Alcohol, Barbiturates (e.g., Seconal, Nembutal), and **Tranquilizers** (e.g., Valium, Librium, Xanax).

Methods of administration:

Oral or injected.

Main effects:

Alcohol at first produces mild euphoria, relaxation, and lowered inhibitions. As dose increases, more of the brain's activity is impaired resulting eventually in sleep, or with increased consumption, even death.

Barbiturates or **"downers"** have a calming, sedative effect; they can reduce inhibitions and promote sleep.

Tranquilizers lower anxiety and also have a calming, sedative effect. They promote relaxation and work with the neurotransmitter **GABA,** which is associated with inhibitory synapses.

Medical uses:

Alcohol can be used as an antiseptic.

Barbiturates are used as sleeping pills or as anticonvulsants.

Tranquilizers are prescribed to lower anxiety.

Side effects:

Impaired coordination, increased urination, emotional swings, depression, impaired judgment, quarrelsomeness, and hangover are some potential side effects of the consumption of **alcohol.**

For **barbiturates,** side effects include impaired coordination and reflexes, and drowsiness.

Side effects of **tranquilizers** are lethargy, sleepiness, and decreased muscular tension.

Potential for addiction/psychological dependence:

Alcohol: High/High.

Barbiturates: High/High.

Tranquilizers: Moderate to High/High.

Withdrawal symptoms:

For **alcohol,** withdrawal symptoms include tremors, nausea, sweating, depression, irritability, and hallucinations.

Withdrawal symptoms for **barbiturates** are trouble sleeping, anxiety, seizures, cardiovascular collapse, and even death.

For **tranquilizers,** restlessness, anxiety, irritability, muscle tension, and trouble sleeping are possible withdrawal symptoms.

5.5.2 Stimulants

Stimulants increase central nervous system activity.

Examples:

Nicotine, Caffeine, Amphetamines (e.g., Benzedrine, Dexedrine, Methadrine), and **Cocaine.**

Methods of administration:

Oral, sniffed, injected, smoked, and freebased.

Main effects:

Nicotine increases metabolic processes (e.g., pulse rate), lowers carbohydrate appetite, and can produce alertness or calmness.

Caffeine promotes wakefulness and increases metabolism but slows reaction times.

Amphetamines (e.g., "speed," "uppers") stimulate neurotransmission at the synapse. Both the central nervous system and the sympathetic branch in the autonomic nervous system are affected. They can increase energy and excitement and reduce fatigue and appetite.

Cocaine increases feelings of excitement and a euphoric mood, boosts energy, and acts as an appetite suppressant.

Medical uses:

Stimulants are used in the treatment of hyperactivity and narcolepsy. **Cocaine** has been used as a local anesthetic.

Side effects:

The main side effects of stimulants include increased pulse and blood pressure, restlessness, reduced appetite, increased sweating and urination, insomnia, and increased aggressiveness.

Potential for addiction/psychological dependence:

Nicotine: High/Moderate to high.

Caffeine: Moderate/Moderate.

Amphetamines: Moderate/High.

Cocaine: Moderate to high/High.

Withdrawal symptoms:

Nicotine: Anxiety, increased appetite, and irritability.

Caffeine: Headache and depression.

Amphetamines: Increased appetite, depression, sleeping for long periods, fatigue, and irritability.

Cocaine: Sleeping for long periods, fatigue, irritability, increased appetite, and depression.

5.5.3 Hallucinogens

Hallucinogens ("psychedelic drugs") are chemical substances that alter perceptions of reality and may cause hallucinations and other distortions in sensory and perceptual experiences.

Examples:

Several synthetic drugs, such as **LSD (lysergic acid diethylamide)** and **PCP (phencyclidine)**, as well as substances extracted from plants, such as **Marijuana.**

Methods of administration:

Smoked, snorted, or swallowed.

Main effects:

LSD is derived from a fungus (**ergot**) that grows on rye. Even small doses (i.e., 10 micrograms) can produce effects that last for hours and include mild euphoria, hallucinations, body image alterations, loss of control of one's attention, and insightful experiences or "mind expansion."

PCP is an **anesthetic** often called **angel dust**. It works by binding to the potassium channels in the brain and muscle-activating neurons. May cause loss of contact with reality, aggressive behavior, hallucinations, and insensitivity to pain.

Marijuana is a mixture of leaves, flowers, and stems from the **hemp** plant. Its active ingredient is **tetrahydrocannabinol** or **THC**. When smoked, THC enters the bloodstream through the lungs and reaches peak concentrations in 10 to 30 minutes and its effects may last for several hours. It generally produces euphoria and relaxation, and in sufficient doses, can produce hallucinations. In addition to being a hallucinogen, marijuana is also a **stimulant at higher doses** and a **depressant at lower doses.**

Medical uses:

Most hallucinogens have no medical uses; marijuana however, has been used in the treatment of glaucoma and to alleviate nausea from chemotherapy. Its use in the treatment of HIV and nausea from chemotherapy is under study.

Side effects:

LSD: Possible panic reactions, anxiety, dilated pupils, paranoia, and jumbled thought processes.

PCP: Violent and bizarre behaviors.

Marijuana: Dry mouth, bloodshot eyes, poor motor coordination, apathy, memory problems, and anxiety.

Potential for addiction/psychological dependence:

LSD: Low/Low.

PCP: Unknown/High.

Marijuana: Low/Moderate.

Withdrawal symptoms:

Possible withdrawal symptoms for the hallucinogens include anxiety, difficulty sleeping, hyperactivity, and decreased appetite.

5.5.4   Narcotics

Narcotics, also referred to as **opiates** or **analgesics,** are used to relieve pain and induce sleep.

Examples:

Opium, Morphine (e.g., Percodan, Demoral), and **Heroine.**

Methods of administration:

Oral, injected, or smoked.

Main effects:

Opium is an unrefined extract of the poppy seed pod.

Morphine is a refined extract of opium and is stronger in its effects.

Heroin is derived from morphine and is even more potent in its pure form.

Because these narcotic drugs are all derived from opium, they reduce pain by blocking neurotransmission. Narcotics appear to reduce pain because they are chemically similar to the body's own natural opiates. They fit into the body's own opiate receptors and mimic their effects thereby stopping pain from reaching the cortex. Immediately after injection, opiates produce a pronounced feeling of intoxication and euphoria, and physical pain is relieved.

Medical uses:

Relief of pain.

Side effects:

The opiates seem to block so many afferent impulses in the brain that not only is pain blocked but also hunger, anxiety, and motivation. Constipation, nausea, and impaired coordination are other possible side effects.

Potential for addiction/psychological dependence:

Opium: High/High.

Morphine: High/High.

Heroin: High/High.

Withdrawal symptoms:

Symptoms of withdrawal from narcotic addiction include diarrhea, chills, sweating, runny nose, muscle spasms, restlessness, and anxiety.

Problem Solving Example:

What are psychoactive drugs? List and define the various types according to their function.

Psychoactive drugs are those that can cause subjective, psychological changes in consciousness. These include alcohol, marijuana, sedatives, stimulants, narcotic drugs, and hallucinogens.

Sedatives or tranquilizers are those drugs that reduce tension and anxiety. Examples of these are resperine and chlorpromazine.

Stimulants or energizers tend to counteract fatigue and produce upswings in mood. Among these drugs are amphetamines ("pep pills"), caffeine, and imipramine.

Narcotic drugs are those that can be used as painkillers. Among these are morphine and heroin. Narcotics are physiologically addictive and dependence on them usually results in a continual increase in dosage.

Hallucinogenic, psychedelic, and psychomimetic are interchangeable terms for drugs whose major feature is the production of hallucinations. These drugs affect the brain functions of perception, cognition (thought processes), and emotion. They may produce pleasurable or depressive reactions and a sense of bodily detachment.

Examples of these are mescaline, psilocybin and LSD (lysergic acid diethylamide, or LSD-25).

Quiz: States of Consciousness

1. The high point of wakefulness is related to

    (A) decrease in body temperature.

    (B) increase in cortisol levels.

    (C) decreased visual alertness.

    (D) All of the above.

2. Generally, as we move from an awake state through deeper stages of sleep, our brain waves _____ in frequency and _____ in amplitude.

    (A) increase; increase

    (B) decrease; decrease

    (C) increase; decrease

    (D) decrease; increase

3. The restorative function theory states that sleep is necessary for

    (A) resting and restoring the body.

    (B) nervous system development.

    (C) consolidating what has been learned during the day.

    (D) All of the above.

4. The uncontrollable, recurring onset of REM sleep is called

    (A) narcolepsy.

    (B) sleep apnea.

    (C) hypersomnia.

    (D) somnambulism.

5. All of the following are theories concerning dreams EXCEPT:

    (A) the activation-synthesis model.

    (B) housekeeping hypothesis.

    (C) automatic writing hypothesis.

    (D) off-line hypothesis.

6. _____ theory states that hypnosis is a splitting of central control of thought processes and behavior.

    (A) State

    (B) Dissociation

    (C) Role

    (D) Split brain

7. Individuals most susceptible to hypnosis tend to have all of the following EXCEPT

    (A) problems with concentration.

    (B) active imaginations.

    (C) proneness to fantasy.

    (D) think highly of hypnosis.

8. In addition to being a hallucinogen, marijuana is also a(n) _____ at higher doses and a _____ at lower doses.

    (A) depressant; stimulant

    (B) stimulant; depressant

    (C) sedative; depressant

    (D) analgesics; stimulant

9. The active ingredient in marijuana is

    (A) phencyclidine.

    (B) diethylamide.

    (C) tetrahydrocannabinol.

    (D) lysergic acid.

10. The potential for addiction/psychological dependence to caffeine is

    (A) low/low

    (B) low/moderate

    (C) moderate/moderate.

    (D) high/high.

ANSWER KEY

1.	(B)	6.	(B)
2.	(D)	7.	(A)
3.	(D)	8.	(B)
4.	(A)	9.	(C)
5.	(C)	10.	(C)

CHAPTER 6

Conditioning and Learning

6.1 Classical Conditioning

Learning is defined as a relative permanent change in our nervous system and behavior as a result of experience, practice, or both. **Conditioning** is the process of forming associations. Learning and conditioning are inferred from behavior because they cannot be observed directly.

Problem Solving Example:

 Define the term "learning."

Learning is a relatively permanent change in behavior resulting from conditions of practice or experience. It is important to use the words "relatively permanent" because transient changes in behavior do not indicate that learning has occurred. (Behavior refers to all the activities an organism engages in, including thought and communication.) Transient changes in behavior are usually spontaneously reversible.

The adjustment of the eyes to different light conditions is a transient change in behavior whereas the learning of basic principles of mathematics is a relatively permanent change in behavior. Learning can be easily distinguished from memory in this case.

A student who learns basic mathematics principles should be able to derive formulae and solve problems whereas the student who has only memorized formulae and certain problem solving procedures will forget them when he stops regularly retrieving them from his memory.

Classical conditioning always involves a **reflexive** or **respondent behavior.** This means that classical conditioning produces an automatic response to a stimulus. **Classical** or **respondent conditioning** occurs when a neutral stimulus that does not trigger a reflexive behavior is **conditioned** so that it will elicit an automatic response. Conditioning occurs because the neutral stimulus has been **associated** with a stimulus that automatically triggers a response.

It appears that both humans and animals may be **biologically prepared** to learn some associations more readily than others. The associations that are more readily learned may be ones that increase chances for survival.

Ivan Pavlov (1849-1936), a Russian physiologist, classically conditioned dogs using the **salivary reflex.** Dogs normally respond to food by salivating. They do *not* have to be conditioned to salivate to food. Dogs do not, however, automatically salivate to the sound of a bell ringing. This is what Pavlov conditioned them to do. He would ring the bell, present the food, and the dogs would salivate. He repeated this procedure until the bell alone would cause the dogs to salivate. They had learned to **associate** the sound of the bell with the presentation of food.

The terms used to describe classical conditioning include:

Unconditioned Stimulus (UCS) — The stimulus that automatically produces a reflex. (In Pavlov's study this was the food.)

Unconditioned Response (UCR) — An automatic response to the UCS; a natural response that does not require conditioning for it to occur. (In Pavlov's study this was salivation to the food.)

Conditioned Stimulus (CS) — A neutral stimulus that does not normally elicit an automatic response; only after pairing it repeatedly with the UCS, does the CS come to elicit a conditioned response. (In Pavlov's study this was the bell.)

Conditioned Response (CR) — The learned response that occurs when the CS is presented alone, without the UCS. (In Pavlov's study, the CR was salivation that occurred to the bell alone; no food was present.)

The standard classical conditioning paradigm is:

		UCS (food)	$\rightarrow$	**UCR** (salivation)
CS (bell)	+	**UCS** (food)	$\rightarrow$	**UCR** (salivation)
		CS alone (bell alone)	$\rightarrow$	**CR** (salivation)

Step 2 is repeated until the CS alone will prompt the CR.

The timing or **temporal relationship** between the conditioned stimulus (CS) and unconditioned stimulus (UCS) can vary:

Forward pairing — CS presented before UCS

Backward pairing — CS presented after UCS

Simultaneous pairing — CS and UCS occur at exactly the same time.

Research has indicated that forward conditioning leads to the best conditioning, especially if the CS precedes the UCS by about half a second. Backward and simultaneous conditioning are much less effective.

After classical conditioning has taken place, the conditioned stimulus (CS) must be paired with or **reinforced** by the unconditioned stimulus (UCS) at least some of the time or else the conditioned response

(CR) will disappear. The process of eliminating the conditioned response (CR) by no longer pairing the unconditioned stimulus (UCS) with the conditioned stimulus (CS) is called **extinction**. Extinction will take place, therefore, if the conditioned stimulus (CS) is presented repeatedly without the unconditioned stimulus (UCS). Extinction is a method that is used intentionally to eliminate conditioned responses (CR).

The conditioned response might recover, however, if a rest period or break follows extinction. A **rest period** would occur if the conditioned stimulus (CS) is *not* presented for a period of time. After this rest period, the very next time the conditioned stimulus (CS) is presented, the conditioned response (CR) is likely to occur (even though it was previously extinguished). If the conditioned response (CR) does reappear, this is called **spontaneous recovery.** Spontaneous recovery is, therefore, the recurrence of a conditioned response (CR) after a rest interval has followed extinction.

Figure 6.1 shows the acquisition, extinction, and spontaneous recovery of a conditioned response (CR).

Reconditioning occurs after extinction has taken place and the conditioned stimulus (CS) and unconditioned stimulus (UCS) are again paired. Learning (i.e., responding with a CR when the CS is presented) is usually quicker during reconditioning than it was during initial conditioning.

Stimulus generalization occurs when a conditioned response (CR) occurs to a stimulus that only **resembles** or is **similar** to the conditioned stimulus (CS) but is *not* identical to it. For instance, Pavlov's dogs were classically conditioned to salivate to a bell (the CS), but if the first time they heard a buzzer they also salivated, this would be stimulus generalization. They were never conditioned with the buzzer, but they responded because the sound resembled that of the bell.

Stimulus discrimination occurs when the differences between stimuli are noticed and, thus, the stimuli are *not* responded to in similar ways. For instance, stimulus discrimination would occur if Pavlov's dogs did *not* salivate to the sound of the buzzer, even if it sounded

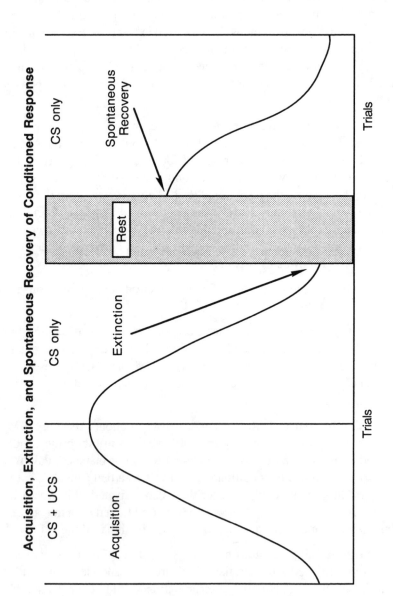

Figure 6.1 Strength of Response

similar to the bell. This would indicate that the dogs could discriminate these two sounds and as a result, responded differently to each.

Researchers have used humans as well as animals in classical conditioning studies. In humans, emotional reactions occur sometimes as a result of classical conditioning because emotions are involuntary, automatic responses. For instance, **phobias** (intense, irrational fears) may develop as a result of classical conditioning.

The most famous classical conditioning study using a human subject was one conducted by American researcher **John Watson** (1878-1958). Although this study is considered unethical today and some have suggested that it is more myth or legend than fact, most textbooks mention the Little Albert study when discussing classical conditioning. Little Albert was an 11-month old infant who initially was not afraid of laboratory white rats. Watson classically conditioned Albert to fear these rats by pairing the presentation of the rat with a loud noise that scared the infant. The diagram of this study would be:

Noise → **Fear response**
(UCS) (UCR)

Rat + **Noise** → **Fear response**
(CS) (UCS) (UCR)

eventually,

Rat alone → **Fear response**
(CS) (CR)

Higher order conditioning occurs when a new neutral stimulus is associated with a conditioned stimulus (CS) and eventually comes to produce the conditioned response (CR). If after Albert was classically conditioned, a dog was always paired with the rat, eventually Albert would display the fear response to the dog. A diagram of this higher order conditioning example would be:

	Rat alone (CS)	→	**Fear** (CR)

Dog + (new stimulus)	**Rat alone** (CS)	→	**Fear** (CR)

eventually,

Dog alone (CS)	→	**Fear** (CR)

Problem Solving Examples:

Q What is classical conditioning? Include a brief explanation of the principal terms used to describe a simple classical conditioning experiment (CS, UCS, CR and UCR).

A Pavlovian, classical (because of Pavlov's now classic experiments) or, the term preferred by many today, respondent conditioning is a simple form of learning in which a subject is conditioned to respond to a new stimulus with an innate or a previously acquired response. In Pavlov's experiments with the salivating response of his dogs he established the basic methodology and terminology still used today in classical conditioning experiments. He knew dogs would salivate when they tasted food. Pavlov referred to the food as the unconditioned stimulus (UCS) because it naturally and consistently elicited salivation, which he called the unconditioned response (UCR).

Pavlov later taught dogs to salivate to light. This was accomplished by presenting a light just prior to presenting the food. After a series of such pairings, the dog would salivate to the light even before food was presented. In this case, the light was a conditioned stimulus (CS) and the salivation to the light was a conditioned response (CR). Pavlov found that he could condition many neutral stimuli to elicit a particular response by repeatedly pairing the neutral stimulus with an UCS.

In classical conditioning, then, the conditioned stimulus (CS) which elicits no response at first, and the unconditioned stimulus (UCS), which consistently evokes a particular response, are presented together to the subject for a number of trials. After some time, the unconditioned stimulus (UCS) can be removed and conditioned stimulus (CS) will elicit a response similar to the unconditioned response (UCR). The subject learns to respond to a stimulus in a way he had not responded before. The subject has been respondently or classically conditioned.

 Give an overview of the historical development of classical conditioning.

As early as 1897, Ivan P. Pavlov (1849-1936), a Russian Nobel prize winner for work on the digestive process, virtually discovered the conditioned response and was the first to investigate it systematically. This phenomenon had been observed before but Pavlov was the first to appreciate its significance. Like many great discoveries, it appeared to be an accidental finding and didn't even seem like much of a discovery at the time. While studying the gastric secretions of dogs in his laboratory, Pavlov noticed that the sound of the footsteps of his associate (who fed the dogs) tended to evoke saliva flow in his dogs. What was curious and interesting to him was that the dogs salivated before the food was put in their mouths. It was of such great interest to him that he stopped his work on gastric secretions and began to study what he called "psychic secretions." He soon discontinued working with the footsteps as a stimulus and began to train his dogs to salivate to a tuning fork or a light.

The essential features of the reflex tradition to which Pavlov belonged have their roots in the work of Descartes, who in the seventeenth century introduced the concept of reflex to describe innate muscle responses following sensory stimuli. Later, Sechenov postulated that the brain operated as a mediator in the reflex process. He termed these "acquired reflexes." Pavlov, accepting Sechenov's definition of an "acquired reflex," saw the possible experimental operation for defining and investigating the "psychic" secretions of his dogs.

Pavlov's terminology is still regarded by investigators of learning as including the most basic descriptive units of behavior and are applicable even in learning paradigms other than classical conditioning. Among his contributions was the introduction of the following terms: conditioning, conditioned stimulus, unconditioned stimulus, reinforcement, stimulus generalization, extinction.

J. B. Watson built upon and expanded Pavlov's work. He applied conditioning principles to emotions, mental disease, language, and learning. In learning, Watson employed the concept of conditioning as a central theoretical construct in which complex learning was considered to be simply the chaining of conditioned reflexes.

The decade following Watson's initial writings saw the broad and largely speculative application of conditioning to a wide range of behaviors, extending from individual behavior to social action. During this period "conditioning" became synonymous with "association" until detailed descriptions of Pavlov's work and reports from more recent research conducted in American laboratories began to reveal the complexities of conditioning. At that time, the prevailing and popular views of the conditioning reflex as a unit of habit and as a substitute for association began to come under strong attack from scientific circles. Nevertheless, these initial views of conditioning have had a strong residual influence on American concepts of conditioning. Specifically, there is still a prevalent tendency to regard any phenomenon deemed associative in nature as "classical conditioning." This term, however, should be reserved for the actual theoretical accounting of such learning experiments (though analogs of classical conditioning from everyday experiences are helpful in initially understanding the phenomenon).

The frequent use of "classical conditioning" as a theoretical term without any substantial body of research using Pavlov's method created the illusion among researchers and the public that Pavlov's findings were complete and well substantiated, which was not true. Consequently, there was a relative neglect of research in classical conditioning until recently.

6.2   Operant and Instrumental Conditioning

In **operant** or **instrumental conditioning,** responses are learned because of their consequences. Unlike classical conditioning, the responses learned in operant/instrumental conditioning are **voluntary.**

There are subtle measurement differences between operant and instrumental conditioning. Because both of these are similar in most respects, however, the term operant conditioning will be used to refer to both.

American psychologist **Edward L. Thorndike's** (1874-1949) **Law of Effect** states that a behavior that is rewarded tends to be repeated, while behavior that is not rewarded takes place only at random. What is learned during operant or instrumental conditioning is that certain responses are instrumental in producing desired effects in the environment.

Reinforcers are consequences for behavior and can be anything that increases the likelihood that a behavior will be repeated. Reinforcers can be positive or negative. Both positive and negative reinforcers have the potential to **increase behaviors. Positive reinforcers** are rewards or other positive consequences that follow behaviors and increase the likelihood that the behaviors will occur again in the future. Giving your dog a biscuit each time he sits on command is an example of positive reinforcement.

Negative reinforcers are anything a subject will work to avoid or terminate. Nagging behaviors are examples of negative reinforcement because parents often will do something to stop the nagging. For instance, a parent who buys a child a candy bar to stop a child's nagging in the grocery store is responding to negative reinforcement. **Escape conditioning** occurs when a subject learns that a particular response will terminate an aversive stimulus. The parent who buys a nagging child candy has escaped the nagging by purchasing candy. **Avoidance conditioning** occurs when a subject responds to a signal in a way that prevents exposure to an aversive stimulus. The candy counter at the store may become a signal that parents should buy candy if they want to avoid or prevent their child's nagging.

Reinforcers can also be primary or secondary. **Primary reinforcers** are necessary to meet biological needs and include such things as food, water, air, etc. **Secondary reinforcers** have acquired value and are not necessary for survival. Grades, money, and a pat on the back are examples of secondary reinforcers.

A reinforcer becomes less effective in promoting future behavior the longer the delay between a behavior and its reinforcement. The declining effectiveness of reinforcement with increasing delay is called the **gradient of reinforcement.**

Extinction can also occur in operant conditioning. The goal is the same as it is in classical conditioning, to decrease or eliminate a response. Extinction occurs in operant conditioning by removing the reinforcer. For example, the dog stops receiving dog biscuits for sitting or the child gets no candy for nagging. Once these reinforcers are removed, both sitting and nagging should decrease and/or be eliminated. **Spontaneous recovery** can also occur in operant conditioning.

How easily an operant response is extinguished is dependent, in part, on how often that response was reinforced or its **schedule of reinforcement.** A **continuous schedule** of reinforcement happens when each and every response is reinforced (100 percent of the time). *Each* time your dog sits on command, he receives a biscuit. Behaviors that are continuously reinforced are easier to extinguish than behaviors that are not reinforced 100 percent of the time.

Behaviors that are *not* reinforced each time they occur are on an **intermittent** or **partial schedule of reinforcement.** There are four possible partial schedules of reinforcement:

Fixed ratio schedule: Reinforcement is given after a fixed number of responses (e.g., every third time your dog sits, he receives a biscuit). Being paid on a piece-rate basis is an example of a fixed ratio schedule. The fixed ratio schedule produces a high rate of responding with a slight pause after each reinforcement is given. Fixed ratio schedules produce the fastest rate of extinction because the subject realizes quickly that reinforcement has stopped.

Variable ratio schedule: Reinforcement is given after a variable number of responses. Thus, on one occasion, reinforcement may occur after 10 responses and on another occasion after 50, etc. The rate of reinforcement depends upon the rate of responding: the faster the response, the more reinforcers received. This schedule produces steady, high rates of responding and is extremely resistant to extinction. Slot machines are based on variable ratio schedules.

Fixed interval schedule: Reinforcement is given after the first response after a given amount of time has elapsed. This may mean a reinforcer every five minutes, for example. Being paid once per month is another example. Fixed interval schedules produce a low rate of responding at the beginning of each interval and a high rate toward the end of each interval.

Variable interval schedule: Reinforcement is given after the first response after a varying amount of time has elapsed. Pop quizzes often occur on a variable interval schedule. The variable interval schedule produces a steady, slow rate of responding.

In general, the ratio schedules produce higher response rates than the interval schedules. Variable schedules are usually harder to extinguish than are fixed schedules because variable schedules are less predictable.

American behaviorist **B. F. Skinner** (1904-1990) devised a chamber, known as a **Skinner box**, to study the effects of various schedules of reinforcement on the behavior of small animals such as rats and pigeons. During **acquisition** or learning, each time a lever in the Skinner box was pressed, a food pellet was dispensed into a food dish. A speaker or light signal was also used to indicate conditions of reinforcement or extinction. In some studies, the grid floor was electrified, and the electric current could be turned off by pressing the lever. The speaker or lights signaled when the current would be turned on and in avoidance trials, the animal had a certain amount of time to press the lever to avoid the shock.

Shaping involves systematically reinforcing closer and closer approximations of the desired behavior. When a rat is first placed in the

Skinner box, it doesn't know that pressing the lever will result in a food reward and may never press the lever on its own. Lever pressing can be conditioned through shaping – each step closer to the lever results in a food reward.

Discriminative stimuli serve as cues that indicate a response is likely to be reinforced. The light in the Skinner box can be a discriminative stimulus. When the light is on, lever pressing results in a food reward. When it is off, lever pressing is not reinforced. The animal will eventually learn to discriminate and to press the lever only when the light is on.

Punishment is also an operant conditioning technique. The goal of punishment is to decrease behavior. Punishment involves the presentation of an **aversive stimulus** or **undesirable consequence** after a behavior has occurred. Something negative can be added or something positive can be taken away. Receiving a ticket for speeding and being placed on house restriction are two examples of punishment.

Timing is very important for punishment to be effective – the sooner the punishment is delivered after the undesired behavior occurred, the better the learning. Even very short delays can reduce the effectiveness of punishment. Punishment must also be **severe** enough to eliminate the undesirable response.

Punishment may have undesirable **side effects.** Punishment often provides a **model of aggressive behavior,** and the person punished may learn that aggression is a method for solving problems. Punishment alone **does not teach appropriate behavior.** The person providing the punishment can become a **feared agent** to be avoided. Punishment can get out of hand and become **abusive.** Many behaviorists today suggest that punishment be avoided as a method used for conditioning. Instead, they recommend the use of extinction to weaken an inappropriate response and reinforcement to increase appropriate behaviors.

Problem Solving Example:

 Describe the differences between classical and operant conditioning.

 Classical and operant conditioning may seem quite similar: both are forms of conditioning, if one withholds the reinforcement or UCS, extinction occurs. Stimulus generalization, discrimination, spontaneous recovery, and higher-order conditioning are properties of both. Indeed the similarities are great; in fact, both types of conditioning are not necessarily mutually exclusive.

The differences, however, are significant. Most of these are procedural in nature.

1. In CC (classical conditioning) the occurrence of a CR is reflexively forced by the UCS (e.g., salivation); in OC (operant conditioning) the response is more voluntary (pressing a bar).

2. In CC the UCS occurs without regard to the subject's behavior; in OC the reward is contingent on the occurrence of a response.

3. CC is preparatory or anticipatory; OC serves to emphasize or guide an organism which already has certain critical responses available.

4. In CC the UCS is the reinforcing stimulus that maintains a response through consistent pairing with a previously neutral stimulus, the CS precedes the UCS; in OC the UCS consists of an incentive, positive or negative, that follows the behavior that is the object of conditioning.

5. In CC the UCS occurs or does not occur independently of whether the CR is made; in OC the reinforcing stimulus is response-contingent.

6. CC is more concerned with what makes one respond and OC focuses on how one responds.

7. Elicited responses represent only a small proportion of the

behavior of higher organisms. The remaining behavior is operant.

8. In CC responses are elicited; in operant conditioning they are emitted.

Distinctions Between Classical Conditioning and Operant Conditioning

---

Classical Conditioning

- Behavior affected is usually experienced as involuntary-for example, reflexes (knee jerk, salivation, eye blink), feelings (fear, anxiety).

- Key events (unconditioned and conditioned stimuli) are presented to the organism.

- Those events elicit the behavior; that is, they directly evoke it.

- In the absence of key stimuli, the behavior does not occur.

Operant Conditioning

- Behavior affected is usually experienced as voluntary – for example, actions (bar press), thoughts (plans for action).

- Key events (reinforcement and punishment) are produced by the organism's behavior.

- Those events control the behavior; that is, they determine how often the organism emits it.

- In the absence of specific stimuli, the behavior does occur; the effect of discriminative stimuli is to alter its frequency.

6.3   Observational Learning

Observational learning occurs when we learn new behaviors by watching others. This is sometimes called **social learning, vicarious conditioning,** or **modeling.**

Observational learning is guided by four processes:

Attention – Attention must be paid to the salient features of another's actions. Prestige or status of a model can influence whether another's actions are noticed.

Retention – Observed behaviors must be remembered in order to be carried out.

Reproduction of Action – We must be able to carry out the behavior that we observed.

Motivation – There must be some reason for carrying out the behavior. Observing someone being rewarded for a behavior increases the likelihood that the behavior will be performed.

Vicarious learning occurs when we learn the relationship between a response and its consequences by watching others. **Vicarious reinforcement** occurs when we observe the model receiving reinforcement. **Vicarious punishment** happens when we observe the model being punished for engaging in a behavior.

Edward Tolman (1886-1959) differentiated between learning and performance. **Latent learning** is learning that is not demonstrated at the time that it occurs. For instance, we may learn a behavior when we observe it, but never display the behavior. Thus, we may learn behavior but never perform it. Tolman maintained that behavior may not be demonstrated until it is motivating to do so.

The classic research on observational learning was conducted by **Albert Bandura** and his colleagues. This research included children watching and imitating an adult's aggressive behavior toward a Bobo doll. Bandura found that children learned the aggressive behavior even when the adult was not reinforced for this behavior. Later research indicated that children who watched an aggressive model being reinforced were much more aggressive in a similar situation than children who saw the model punished for the aggressive actions. Through his research, Bandura has demonstrated that both classical and operant conditioning can take place through observational learning — by observing another's conditioning.

Problem Solving Example:

 Discuss the four processes involved in observational learning according to Bandura and Walters.

 Starting from the premise that most complex human behaviors are learned through verbal transmission and information and through observation of a skilled model, Bandura and Walters have devoted much time and research to the investigation of the process by which learning occurs through observation. This process is also called "modeling."

They have observed four processes through which this type of learning occurs:

(1) Attention process – Exposure alone does not assure that learning will occur: it is also necessary that the learner pay attention to the model. Several variables have been found to affect learner attention including the distinctiveness and likeability of the model, the past history of reinforcement of the observer for attending to similar models, the psychological state of the observer, and the complexity of the behavior to be modeled.

(2) Retention process – The observer must have the capacity to recall what the model did.

(3) Reproduction process – The observer then must use memory to guide an actual performance. The student driver may recall the steps he observed in learning to parallel park: "Line the front wheels of your vehicle with the back wheels of the car in the space in front of the one into which you are going to park." Even with correct recall the performance will be influenced by the physical abilities of the learner. If a teacher is with the learner and is able to give feedback on parts of the parking process that have been incorrectly retained or for which a particular skill needs to be refined, the learning will take place more rapidly. Thus, abilities and feedback are important guiding processes during a learning experience.

(4) Motivational process – Although an individual may have acquired and retained the observed behavior, he will not translate it into behavior if that behavior is punishing. The student driver will find himself avoiding the need to parallel park if the first few times he tries it other drivers honk impatiently or yell at him for holding up traffic.

If, on the other hand, the attempts at parking yield successful results or are reinforced by the encouragement of another person, the learner may be positively motivated to manifest the behavior he has learned.

CHAPTER 7

Human Memory

7.1 Encoding

Memory is the storing of information over time. **Encoding** is the process of placing information into memory. **Storage** is the process of retaining information in memory. Getting information out of memory is called **retrieval.**

You must pay attention to the information that you want to place or **encode** in your memory.

Fergus Craik and **Robert Lockhart** proposed three levels for encoding incoming information. They suggested that whether we remember information for a few seconds or a lifetime depends on how deeply we process the information. Information can be processed or encoded according to three different features:

Structural – Information is stored based on visual codes – what information "looks" like or its physical structure.

Phonemic – Information is stored based on acoustic codes – what it sounds like.

Semantic – Information is stored based on semantic codes – what it means. Most information appears to be stored in memory based semantic codes.

Levels of processing theory suggests that deeper levels of processing result in longer-lasting memory codes. The *deepest level* of processing appears to be semantic. Structural encoding is often a shallow level of processing and phonemic encoding is intermediate.

Allan Paivio's dual code theory suggests that information is better remembered when it is represented in both semantic and visual codes because this allows for storage of both the word and image.

7.2 Storage

The **information processing theories** of memory emphasize how information flows through a series of separate memory stores. One prominent information processing model that was proposed by **Richard Atkinson** and **Richard Shiffrin** describes this flow of information through the **sensory memory** to **short-term memory** and finally to **long-term memory**. This model is described below and is presented in Figure 7.1.

7.2.1 Sensory Memory

Sensory memory (sometimes referred to as **sensory register**) holds sensory information for a brief period after the physical stimulus is no longer available. It holds an exact copy of the sensory stimulus for only a few seconds. More information enters our sensory memory than will reach our short-term memory. **George Sperling** developed a **partial report procedure** to measure this. Subjects were to report only some of the items from a visual display that they saw for a very short period of time (e.g., 1/10th of a second). Sperling found that subjects were able to see more items than they could report and that subjects' memories of the visual display faded completely after about one second.

In general, sensory memory holds information just long enough to recognize and transfer it to short-term memory for further processing through a process called **selective perception** or **selective attention**. Selective perception/attention allows only specific information out of the many possible sensory messages bombarding us at any one time to enter into our conscious awareness. It is controlled by the focus of our

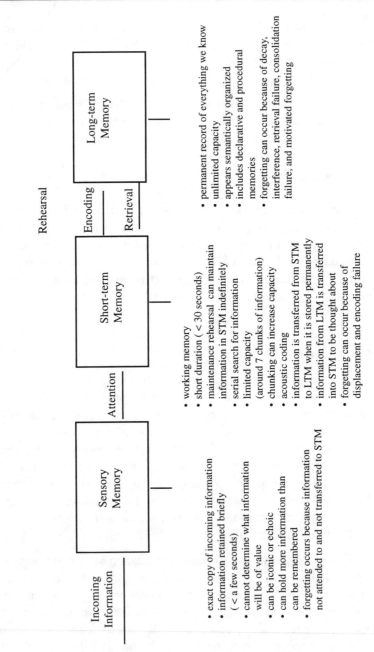

Figure 7.1 Multi-Store Model of Human Memory

Incoming
Information

Rehearsal

Sensory
Memory

Attention

Short-term
Memory

Encoding

Retrieval

Long-term
Memory

- exact copy of incoming information
- information retained briefly
  (< a few seconds)
- cannot determine what information
  will be of value
- can be iconic or echoic
- can hold more information than
  can be remembered
- forgetting occurs because information
  not attended to and not transferred to STM

- working memory
- short duration (< 30 seconds)
- maintenance rehearsal can maintain
  information in STM indefinitely
- serial search for information
- limited capacity
  (around 7 chunks of information)
- chunking can increase capacity
- acoustic coding
- information is transferred from STM
  to LTM when it is stored permanently
- information from LTM is transferred
  into STM to be thought about
- forgetting can occur because of
  displacement and encoding failure

- permanent record of everything we know
- unlimited capacity
- appears semantically organized
- includes declarative and procedural
  memories
- forgetting can occur because of decay,
  interference, retrieval failure, consolidation
  failure, and motivated forgetting

attention and the set of expectancies we have prior to receiving the information.

Iconic sensory memories (or **icons**) are visual representations that last for only about one second in sensory memory. **Echoic sensory memories** (or **echoes**) are representations of sound sensory memories that may last for several seconds.

7.2.2 Short-Term Memory

Short-term memory (STM) is where conscious thinking and processing of information take place. Whatever you are thinking about right now is in your short-term memory.

Once information enters short-term or **"working memory,"** it usually remains there for only about 20 to 30 seconds because short-term memory is very sensitive to interruption or interference. **John Brown** and **Margaret Peterson** devised a method for measuring the duration of short-term memory. Subjects were presented with a stimulus and then asked to count backwards. This backward counting prevented active rehearsal of the previously presented stimulus. Brown and the Petersons found that by 20 seconds of backward counting, subjects could not remember the previously presented stimulus.

Unless the information is important and meaningful or is being actively **rehearsed** or repeated, it quickly leaves short-term memory and is "forgotten" when new information **displaces** it as we begin to think about something else. The material is forgotten because it was never learned. **Displacement** occurs, therefore, when new information enters short-term memory and pushes out existing material. For example, when you look up a number in a phone directory and dial it once, it is doubtful that you will "remember" the number at a later date. You held the number in your short-term memory while dialing. Within 20 seconds after dialing, however, the number was no longer consciously available and was "forgotten" as you began to think about something else.

In order to determine if certain information is in short-term memory, researchers have proposed that we could engage in a **parallel search** by examining all the information in short-term memory at once, or we could use a **serial search,** examining only one bit of information at a time. Research results indicate that the search process in short-term memory is serial.

Short-term memory is also limited in the amount of information it can hold. The average adult can hold between five to nine bits or **chunks** of information in short-term memory. **George Miller** proposed the **magical number seven, plus or minus two** as the capacity of short-term memory. The capacity of short-term memory can be increased by using bigger chunks of information or by what Miller referred to as **chunking.** Chunking involves organizing or grouping separate bits of information into larger units or chunks. For example, 5 8 1 2 7 8 6 3 could be chunked into 58 12 78 63. This transforms eight bits of information into four, thereby freeing up space in short-term memory.

Memory span is a measure of the capacity of short-term memory. It is the largest number of items that can be recalled perfectly from short-term memory after only one presentation and no time for study.

Although various types of memory codes can be used in short-term memory, it appears that **acoustic coding** dominates, especially for verbal information.

Information in short-term memory may be new information coming in from the sensory store or it may be old information coming in from long-term memory in order to be thought about and used.

7.2.3 Long-Term Memory

If *enough* repeated rehearsal or practice occurs, information may be transferred from short-term memory into long-term memory. **Long-term memory (LTM)** is our permanent storehouse of information. For instance, all the knowledge we have accumulated, all the skills we have learned, and all of our memories of past experiences are stored in our long-term memories. The more meaningful the information is, the more easily it can be stored in long-term memory. Some information is stored automatically from short-term memory into long-term memory without effort, usually because this information is highly meaningful. Most information, however, must be actively rehearsed in order to be transferred from short-term to long-term memory.

Unlike short-term memory, long-term memory appears to have unlimited storage capacity.

Information in long-term memory appears to be organized. Research has suggested that new facts are learned by fitting them into a network of pre-existing knowledge.

Propositional network theory suggests that we store meanings in propositional representations in long-term memory. A **proposition** is the smallest unit of information that makes sense. Each proposition is represented by an oval or circle, called a node, which is connected to the components of the proposition by arrows, called **links.** For instance, the proposition "dog" might be connected to the nodes "bark," "fur," and "four legs."

Research shows that there are at least two broad types of memory circuits in long-term memory:

Declarative Memory — "Fact" memories such as names, dates, events; related to thinking and problem solving; accessible to conscious awareness; can often be rapidly learned and rapidly forgotten; has been subdivided into **semantic memory** (store of factual information) and **episodic memory** (store of our personal or autobiographical experiences).

Procedural Memory — "Skill" memory such as remembering how to ride a bike, play a musical instrument, or eat with a fork; learned by repetition and practice and are hard to unlearn; often performed without conscious thought.

Some long-term memories seem to be visual. An extreme and rather rare example is **eidetic memory.** Eidetic memory is characterized by relatively long-lasting and detailed images of scenes that can be scanned as if they were physically present. They are rare in adults and occur more frequently during childhood.

Human memory is so complicated that long-term memory storage and retrieval do not appear to be limited to just one brain structure, although the exact process is not completely understood. When a memory is stored, communication at existing synapses is improved, and the structure of neuron parts near the synapse is changed. Research has shown that the **hippocampus** is somehow important in storing and retrieving memories, as are the **amygdala** and the **thalamus.** The hippocampus, amygdala, and thalamus all send nerve fibers to the **cerebral cortex,** and it is in the cortex that memories are probably stored.

Neurotransmitters are also important in memory. For example, patients with **Alzheimer's** disease have decreased amounts of the neurotransmitter **acetylcholine.** Drugs that interfere with acetylcholine neurotransmission impair memory. Drugs that increase its production sometimes improve memory.

Problem Solving Example:

Briefly describe the three stage theory of memory processing.

Our ability to remember depends upon a complex information processing system. Researchers have suggested that there are at least three stages of memory which are distinguished on the basis of storage time. Immediate (sensory) memory lasts for about one second, short-term memory lasts for several minutes, and long-term memory is thought to be permanent. Each memory stage involves different processes and is affected by time, interference and inhibition factors.

Immediate (sensory) memory has been described as a bridge between perception and memory. Sperling's (1960) and Averbach and Cornell's (1961) experiments have supported the theory of immediate memory, which refers to a brief afterimage of the stimulus itself. Immediate memory may give one the opportunity to organize and categorize what was seen, which is essential for a more permanent memory.

Short-term memory refers to what a person remembers for several seconds after an experience. Short-term memory is a temporary process that holds the trace of an experience for a limited amount of time or until a more permanent trace can be established in long-term memory.

Short-term memory is susceptible to both interference processes and the effects of time.

Long-term memory is the permanent record of the experience. The storage of items in long-term memory is affected not by the passage of time but by interference processes. Items enter long-term memory through a rehearsal process which occurs in short-term memory.

Items which are not rehearsed in short-term memory are usually lost and cannot enter the long-term memory store.

7.2.4 Mnemonics

Mnemonics are strategies for remembering information. They work because they add meaning and context to hard-to-remember information. Several different mnemonics are described below:

Rehearsal – Repeating (or writing or reading) the information over and over. This is a primitive method for remembering. Other methods are more effective and efficient.

Elaboration – Thinking about how new material is connected or related to information already in long-term memory. This results in deeper levels of processing than simple rehearsal.

Method of Loci – Used to remember a list of items. Think of a familiar path or route and then visualize each item you have to remember at different locations along this path or route. For instance, you could visualize one item in your driveway, another in your garage, another at your door, etc.

Peg Word System – Can be used to remember a list of items in a set order. First, you memorize a list of words that will serve as "memory pegs" (such as "one is a bun," "two is a shoe") and then you create a visual image between the peg word and what you need to remember. For instance, if you need to remember the terms "dog and tree," you could visual a dog in between a hot dog bun and a Christmas tree that is decorated with old tennis shoes.

Organization – Reorganizing information into meaningful

groupings. For instance, organizing spelling words for study based on identical prefixes.

SQ3R – Series of five steps that can be used to learn reading material. These steps include surveying, questioning, reading, reciting, and reviewing. This is also known as the **PQRST method:** preview, question, read, self-recitation, and test.

Overlearning – Studying or practicing material beyond mastery – beyond the point where it can be repeated or carried out without error.

Metamemory – An effective way to improve one's memory is to become aware of it. Metamemory is our awareness of memory – how it works, its limitations, strategies for remembering, etc.

Spaced Practice – Short study sessions spread out over an extended period of time lead to better learning than does **massed practice** (one long learning or cramming session).

7.3　Retrieval

Retrieval involves bringing information from long-term memory to short-term memory so that it can be used or examined. Thus, whenever we remember anything, we are *retrieving* that memory from where it is stored. Retrieval is generally preceded by an internal process called **memory search.**

Retrieval cues help us gain access to a memory and can be any stimulus or bit of information that aids in the retrieval of information from long-term memory.

Two basic methods of measuring retrieval are:

Recall – Material must be remembered with few or no retrieval cues (e.g., essay tests).

Recognition – Task is loaded with retrieval cues; material must be remembered through identification of the correct response (e.g., multiple-choice tests).

Encoding specificity principle states that retrieval cues are more efficient when they are coded when the information is learned, and that retrieval success is most likely if the context at the time of retrieval approximates that during encoding. For instance, people remember more material when their psychological state or physical location are similar to what they were when the material was originally learned. This is referred to as **state dependent** and **locus dependent learning,** respectively. According to **locus dependent learning** we should study or learn in a location or context that is as similar as possible to where we will be tested in order to maximize retrieval cues. The same is true of psychological state. If we are in a happy state when we learn material, we will be more likely to retrieve this information in the future if we are happy according to **state dependent learning.**

It is easier to retrieve beginning and ending items in a list and most difficult to remember the middle items. Recall being better for items at the beginning and end of a sequence is known as the **serial position effect.** Information at the beginning of a sequence is likely to be retrieved because it has already been placed in long-term memory. This is known as the **primacy effect.** Information at the end of the sequence is likely to still be in short-term memory and easily recalled, known as the **recency effect.** Middle items are least likely to be retrieved because they are neither in long-term memory nor in short-term memory.

The **tip-of-the-tongue experience** occurs when we are confident that we know information but cannot retrieve it. Even though the correct information cannot be recalled, it often can be recognized. This is because recognition tests provide retrieval cues about the needed information.

Problem Solving Example:

Describe a typical information processing sequence model.

There are many highly sophisticated information processing models available. The following is a brief and general outline of the major stages that might be included in a typical model that explains how the human perceptual and cognitive systems process the flow of stimulation from the environment.

Stage 1: iconic or echoic storage. This stage represents a fleeting experience that is of great importance in the study of information processing. In the visual realm the iconic image is that which occurs during a single glance. Usually lasting approximately 1/15 of a second, iconic storage consists of a series of successive glances, each representing a small section of a larger object. In hearing, the duration of different echoic codes is less distinct, but each code is a sample of a larger auditory event.

Stage 2: image representation or encoding. The momentary sensory experience provides an abundance of information that when combined with other experiences can lead to the recognition of a particular image or sound. For example, momentary glances provide color, texture, density, movement and shape. At stage two this information would be examined and compared. Essential features would be extracted so that the pattern might be recognized as the word "car." By the encoding of this word, other information such as color, brightness, and shape can be discarded.

Stage 3: storage: Short-term memory. It is here that the encoded information resides until it can combine with information coming from the next moment or until it can be transferred to long-term memory. Short-term memory has a limited capacity; it can usually store up to about 8 items.

Stage 4: storage: Long-term memory. Not all information is finally stored in long-term memory. But whatever memory is not within short-term memory can be said to be in long-term memory where it is available for use as needed.

Attention processes play an important role in determining whether information will be transferred from short to long-term memory.

7.4 Forgetting

There are several theories that attempt to explain why forgetting occurs:

Decay Theory – If information in long-term memory is not used, it gradually fades over time until it is lost completely.

Interference Theory – Information in long-term memory is forgotten because other learning gets in the way of what needs to be remembered. Two types of interference have been described: **Proactive interference** occurs when old information in long-term memory interferes with remembering new information. **Retroactive interference** occurs when new memories interfere with remembering old memories.

Retrieval Failure – Not enough retrieval cues are available to prompt remembering. Memory still exists, but there is no suitable cue to trigger it.

Encoding Failure – The information was never learned; that is, the information never made it from short-term memory into long-term memory for permanent storage.

Consolidation Failure – Memories new to long-term memory take time to consolidate or be firmly implanted. Any disruption in the consolidation process can prevent a permanent memory from forming. Examples include a grand mal seizure, blow to the head, or anything that causes the loss of consciousness. **Retrograde amnesia** is the term used to describe a loss of memory for events occurring for periods of time *prior* to a brain injury. **Anterograde amnesia** is used to describe a loss of memory for events that occurred *after* a brain injury.

Motivated Forgetting – This occurs when disturbing, anxiety producing, or otherwise unpleasant memories are no longer consciously available because it would be disturbing to remember them. We tend to remember pleasant events better than unpleasant ones.

Hermann Ebbinghaus (1850-1909) was the first to plot a

forgetting curve. He personally memorized lists of **nonsense syllables** (consonant-vowel-consonant trigrams, such as "wuf" and "rit") and later tested his own recall. He found that the longer the list of nonsense syllables, the more learning trials required. Ebbinghaus also found that most forgetting occurs immediately after learning, and then the rate of forgetting slows down considerably. This is what his forgetting curve documents. Ebbinghaus also measured **savings** or the finding that re-learning the same material is quicker and easier the second time. The concept of savings is used as evidence that forgetting is never complete.

CHAPTER 8

Language and Thought

8.1 Major Properties of Spoken Language

Language and thinking are two abilities that make us uniquely human.

A spoken language requires the use of **signs** and **symbols** within a **grammar.** Grammar determines how the various signs and symbols are arranged and is a set of rules for combining the symbols or **words** into sentences. Language also allows us to use the signs and symbols within our grammar to create novel constructions.

Some characteristics of spoken language include:

Phonemes – The smallest unit of sound that affects the meaning of speech. The English language consists of 53 phonemes. By changing the beginning phoneme, the word "hat" comes "cat."

Morphemes – The smallest unit of language that has meaning. When speaking of more than one bat, we add the morpheme "s." Morphemes are often referred to as roots, stems, prefixes, and suffixes. Words are usually sequences of morphemes but one morpheme can constitute a whole word.

Semantics – The study of meaning in language.

Syntax – The set of rules that determine how words are combined to make phrases and sentences.

Phonetics – The study of how sounds are put together to make words.

Grammar – A broader term than syntax; it includes both syntax and phonetics.

Pragmatics – Includes the social aspects of language, including politeness, conversational interactions, and conversational rules.

Psycholinguistics – The study of the psychological mechanisms related to the acquisition and use of language.

Noam Chomsky distinguished between a sentence's **surface structure** (the words actually spoken) and its **deep structure** (its underlying meaning).

Two sentences, therefore, could have different surface structures but similar deep structures. An example would be, "The dog bit the boy" and "The boy was bitten by the dog." The surface structure of a sentence could also have more than one deep structure (e.g., "Visiting relatives can be boring."). When we hear a spoken sentence, we do not retain the surface structure, but instead transform it into its deep structure. Chomsky referred to this theory as **transformational grammar theory.**

Speech perception is guided by both bottom-up and top-down perception. **Bottom-up processing** in perception depends on the information from the senses at the most basic level, with sensory information flowing from this low level upward to the higher, more cognitive levels. For instance, the phoneme "c" in the word "cat" is perceived, in part, because our ears gather precise information about the characteristics of this sound. **Top-down processing** emphasizes the kind of information stored at the highest level of perception and includes concepts, knowledge, and prior knowledge. We are so skilled at top-down processing, for example, that we sometimes believe that we hear a missing phoneme. **Warren** and **Warren** found that subjects reported they heard the word "heel" in the following sentence where the * indicates a coughing sound: "It was found that the *eel was on the shoe." Subjects thought they heard the phoneme "h" even though the correct sound vibration never reached their ears. This is an example of top-down processing because prior knowledge and expectations influenced what subjects perceived they had heard.

8.2 Language Development

An outline of language development follows:

Cooing and Crying

↓

Babbling

↓

One-word Stage

↓

Two-word Stage

↓

Telegraphic Speech

↓

Verb Tenses, Meaning Modifiers, Pronouns, etc. Added

↓

Syntax Acquired

The first vocalizations that infants make include cooing and crying. At about four months of age, infants begin to **babble.** Their babblings are comprised of a repetition of syllables (e.g., "mamamama").

By six months of age, an infant is more likely to babble when an adult is talking to the infant. Babbling appears to be an innate ability because deaf infants usually babble.

Infants usually begin to understand several individual words that caregivers are saying by five to eight months of age. A child's first words are ordinarily spoken between 10 to 12 months of age. This is referred to as the **one-word stage** because they can usually only use one word at a time. The first words that children use tend to be concrete nouns and verbs. Children often underextend and overextend the meanings of their first words. **Underextension** occurs when a child only uses a word in a specific context (e.g., only says "duck" when in the bathtub with a toy duck but never refers to this toy by name when outside the bathtub). **Overextension** or **overgeneralization** occurs when a child uses a word to mean more than an adult speaker would. For instance, a child who calls *all* four-legged, furry animals (cats, dogs, etc.) "doggie" is overextending or overgeneralizing.

Some researchers have referred to children's one-word utterances as **holophrases** — that is, this one word could be interpreted to mean an entire phrase. For instance, a child points at an object and says "Cookie." This one-word could possibly mean, depending on context, "I want a cookie," "There is a cookie," or "Is that a cookie?"

Children from 18 to 20 months of age are in the **two-word stage** of language development because they are now making short, two-word sentences (e.g., "More milk," "Where ball?"). Their vocabulary is also expanding rapidly during this stage. They may learn several new words each day.

Telegraphic speech quickly follows the two-word stage and consists of sentences that do not contain any morphemes, conjunctions, prepositions, or any other **function words.** Telegraphic speech only contains the **content words** necessary to convey meaning, similar to a telegram (e.g., "Doggie kiss Jeff."). Children's first sentences follow the subject-verb-object sequence, and children often rely on this word order to make their meaning clear.

Eventually, children add verb endings, adjectives, auxiliary verbs, and morphemes to their utterances. Interestingly, initially children tend to use the correct verb tenses, even the exceptions (e.g., "went," "ran"). By age four or five, however, they are often using incorrect forms ("goed," "runned"). These errors seem to indicate that children are acquiring general rules about their language and for a period of time they overgeneralize these rules to the exceptions. Eventually children use the exceptions appropriately.

By age five, children have acquired most of the syntax of their native language.

When speaking to infants and older language-learning children, older children and adults typically use **motherese**. Motherese is speech that contains short sentences that are often repeated. This speech tends to consist of concrete nouns and active verbs. Pronouns, adjectives, conjunctions, and past tenses are usually absent. The sentences are enunciated clearly, often in a high-pitched voice. Many researchers believe that motherese helps children learn language.

An ongoing **nature vs. nurture** debate has been whether language is basically an innate, biological process or a learned phenomenon.

Many researchers hold the view that children are somehow biologically programmed to learn language. According to Chomsky, the **language acquisition device** gives children an *innate* ability to process speech and to understand both the fundamental relationships among words and the regularities of speech. Although imitation, correction, and environment influence speech acquisition, much evidence suggests that it is a product of maturation. Researchers have also proposed a **critical period** for language learning during childhood. If exposed to language during this critical period, language learning will take place. After the critical period, language learning will be more difficult.

B. F. Skinner and other learning theorists proposed that language learning takes place similar to other forms of learning described in Chapter 6. That is, parents selectively reinforce and shape babbling sounds into words. When parents speak to their children, children receive attention and often affection as well. Children then try to make these reinforcing word sounds themselves and try to imitate their parents because it is reinforcing to do so.

Problem Solving Examples:

Q Trace language development during preschool age.

A During preschool age, the language development of the child progresses beyond the formation of two-word sentences. He begins to form three-word sentences and, from this point on, his language and grammar become more diverse and complex. Three-word sentences are formed by combining pairs of two-word sentences. For example, "The big." and "The boy." combine to form "The big boy." During early preschool age the child also learns some ordering rules. He learns to order adjectives by correctly saying a sentence such as, "The two blue cars," rather than "The blue two cars."

During this period, word classes differentiate into subclasses and the child eventually incorporates and uses all the parts of speech in language: noun, verb, adjective, etc.

During the third year, the child learns transformations. He can take a simple declarative sentence and transform it into a command, a question, or a negative. By applying the transformational rules that he has now incorporated, he can transform a sentence such as "He goes," into "Did he go?" or "He did not go." The child is now at a much more advanced stage than in infancy when he merely attached the word "no" to the beginning or end of a sentence to form the negative.

During preschool age, the child learns the proper use of articles as well as the proper time to use singular or plural nouns. He learns that "a box" is correct but "a money" isn't; he begins to understand that "two men" is proper pluralization, not "two mans."

Vocabulary becomes more extensive during the preschool period. By age 4, the child has a vocabulary of well over 1,000 words.

Q Discuss the role language plays in the intellectual development of the preschool child.

A Several studies indicate that the level of linguistic ability in children is related to the level of intellectual ability. As the child's capacity to use language increases, his level of intelligence increases. The increase in intelligence facilitates the further development of language. Research shows that language ability is an important factor in discrimination and dimensional learning. Studies have shown that discrimination learning (the ability to distinguish one object from another) is easier to the subject if the objects are both well known and have names with which the subject is familiar. In addition, attributing names to unfamiliar objects facilitates discrimination in the child.

Pyles (1932) concluded that verbalization facilitates learning. Employing 80 children as subjects, whose ages ranged from two to seven, Pyles tested the effect of language on discrimination learning. In her experiment, Pyles presented the children with five different animal forms. Underneath one animal she hid a toy. The child had to select which animal covered the toy. In one situation, the animal forms were named and were familiar to the children. In another variation, Pyles used unfamiliar and unnamed animal forms. In the third variation, unfamiliar forms were used but names were ascribed to each of them. Pyles found that only 54 percent of the children tested were able to distinguish successfully among the five animal forms when they were unfamiliar and unnamed, but 72 percent were able to distinguish among unfamiliar forms when names were ascribed to them. Hence, Pyles concluded that language facilitates learning.

Bruner (1966) has shown that the child's level of thinking is also related to his linguistic ability. In one of his experiments (with Kenney, 1966), Bruner used a tray or matrix of nine glasses of three different heights and widths. In this test of transposition, children between the ages of 5 and 7 were asked to perform one of three tasks: restore the glasses on the tray to their original order; replace missing glasses from the pattern; or rearrange the matrix by transposing glasses of the diagonal corners. The subjects were asked to describe the matrix as they originally found it and the condition of the matrix after they rearranged it. Bruner and Kenney's subjects voiced three types of descriptions. The youngest subjects employed global descriptions. These subjects used words that conveyed size: "bigger," "littler," "gianter," "smaller." Dimensional descriptions were used by older children. A typical dimensional description might sound like the following: "This one is smaller and thinner while that one is taller and fatter." Some subjects used a third type of verbal description, labeled confounded, because it combined dimensional and global terms; that is, both words of size and dimensional words. Bruner and Kenney concluded that children who used dimensional description were more successful at transposing the glasses than those children who used confounded or global terms. Therefore, language and thinking levels are directly related.

 What is the Language Acquisition Device (LAD)? Describe how it works.

During the third year of life a child learns syntax (the rules of grammar). Chomsky (1957, 1965) proposed a theory to explain the acquisition of syntax. He believes that children are born with a certain "something," a certain gene predisposition that enables them to learn grammar. This is called a Language Acquisition Device (LAD) or an Acquisition Machine (AM). This "something" exists at birth. Chomsky used this concept to explain the relative ease with which the normal child learns grammar. He also uses it to explain why most children make few grammatical mistakes when learning syntax.

Chomsky's LAD theory has neither been proved nor disproved. Although some linguists tend to question the theory (presumably for its vagueness), a better explanation has yet to be devised which can account for the rapid acquisition of syntactic rules during the third and fourth years. Imitation is not a good explanation because the child often makes grammatical mistakes which he could not have picked up from others. Rather than mere imitation, the child learns certain rules that become ingrained in his psyche. He knows, for example, that to indicate the plural tense, he should add "s" to the end of a word. He may not know, however, that this is not the correct procedure in every case. He might say, for example, "oxes" rather than "oxen."

Until a better explanation is provided for syntax acquisition, the subject will remain a source of conjecture and debate.

8.3 Elements of Thought

Thinking is defined as the manipulation of mental representations. **Cognition** includes the mental activities involved in the acquisition, storage, retrieval, and use of knowledge.

John Watson proposed that thinking is merely subvocal speech and is not a mental activity. He felt that we talk to ourselves *so quietly* that it is not apparent that we are doing so. Other researchers have confirmed that thinking is *not* subvocal speech. For instance, individuals who cannot speak can think.

8.3.1 Concepts

A basic element of thought is the notion of concepts. A **concept** is a label that represents a class or group of objects, people, or events that share common characteristics or qualities. We organize our thinking by using concepts, and concepts allow us to think about something new by relating it to a concept we already know. Concept packages are called schemas.

Some concepts are well-defined, and each member of the concept has all of the defining properties; no nonmember does. These are sometimes referred to as **artificial concepts**. An example of an artificial concept would be "registered voters" – you either are or are not registered to vote.

Other concepts are not so clearly defined but are encountered in our everyday life. These **natural concepts** have no set of defining features but instead have characteristic features – members of this concept must have at least some of these characteristics. "Bird" is a natural concept. **Prototypes** are objects or events that best represent a natural concept. A sparrow or robin would be considered prototypical birds by many individuals. New concepts are easier to learn if they are organized around a prototype or schema.

8.3.2 Mental Imagery

Mental imagery refers to mental representations of things that are not physically present. Research has shown that imagery can play an important role in thinking. Some psychologists believe that thinking with mental images differs from thinking with words, just as pictures differ from sentences.

Some psychologists feel that we store mental images based on an **analog code** or a representation that closely resembles the physical object. Others argue that mental images are stored based on **propositions** or in terms of abstract descriptions and these descriptions are used to create an image.

Roger Shepard and **Jacqueline Metzler** reported evidence that supports the analog view of mental imagery. They found that it took subjects longer to rotate an object 180 degrees than to rotate it 20 degrees, just as it takes longer to rotate physical objects a greater distance. **Stephen Kosslyn** found that subjects make judgments about mental images in the same way that they make judgments about an actual picture. That is, it took them longer to make judgments about small mental images than about large ones. Forming large mental images took longer than forming small ones. These results also support the analog view.

Cognitive maps contain our mental images of what is where. They are mental representations of particular spatial arrangements. For instance, you probably have a cognitive or mental map of the United States, as well as one for your state, your town, your campus, your house, etc. Cognitive maps are not accurate copies of the environment but instead represent each individual's perspective. Researcher **E. C. Tolman** reported that even laboratory rats appear to form cognitive maps. As a result of experience in a maze, they seemed to develop a mental awareness of not only the physical space in the maze but also the elements within the space. The rats used their cognitive maps to locate food even when the usual path to the food was blocked.

8.3.3 Reasoning

Reasoning involves transforming information to reach a conclusion. It includes evaluating and generating arguments to reach a conclusion.

Inductive reasoning involves reasoning from the specific to the general. For example, drawing conclusions about all members of a category or concept based on only some of the members is inductive reasoning. **Deductive reasoning** is reasoning from the general to the specific. Making a prediction based on a theory involves deductive reasoning.

Logical reasoning includes mental procedures that yield valid conclusions. Formal tasks have been developed that measure logical reasoning. Two such tasks are **syllogisms** and **analogies.**

Syllogisms are arguments made up of two propositions, called **premises,** and a conclusion based on these premises. They require deductive reasoning.

For example, is the following reasoning valid?

"All cats are animals."

"All cats have four legs."

"Therefore, all animals have four legs." No, the reasoning is not valid. There are some animals which do not have four legs.

An **analogy** is a type of reasoning task that is always made up of four parts. The relationship between the first two parts is the same as the relationship between the last two. Analogies require inductive reasoning. For example:

"*Light* is to *dark* as *summer* is to _____." Light is the opposite of dark, therefore, summer is the opposite of winter.

8.4 Problem Solving

Problem solving is the mental activity used when we want to reach a certain goal that is not readily available.

Problem solving includes:

Understanding the problem.

Planning a solution.

Carrying out the solution.

Evaluating the results.

Problem representation or the way you think about a problem can make it easier or harder to solve. We can represent problems visually, verbally, with symbols (e.g., mathematically), or concretely with objects. A chart or **matrix** that represents all possible combinations of solutions could also be used to keep track of what solution has been and has not been tried.

Some problem-solving strategies include:

Algorithms – Every possible solution is explored. Guarantees problem will be solved eventually, although can be time consuming.

Heuristics – "Rules of thumb" or shortcuts that help solve problems. They seem to offer the most reasonable approach to reaching the goal. However, there is no guarantee that a solution will be reached.

Subgoals or Means-ends Analysis – Intermediate steps for solving a problem. Part of the problem is solved with each subgoal. Often not obvious how to divide problem into subgoals.

Analogy – Solution to an earlier problem is used to help solve current problem. Often difficult to recognize similarity between problems, however.

Working Backwards – For a problem with a well-specified goal, you begin at the goal and work backwards. Worth considering when working forward has not been successful.

Expert Systems or Artificial Intelligence – Computer programs that solve specific problems. Most use algorithms.

Incubation – Putting the problem aside for a while and engaging in some other activity before returning to the problem.

Trial and Error – One solution after another is tried in no particular order until a solution is found. Can be very time consuming.

Some problem solving problems include:

Functional Fixedness – The inability to solve a problem because the function we assign to objects tends to remain fixed or stable. We tend to see objects only in terms of their customary functions. Adversely affects problem solving and creativity.

Mental Set – Tendency to persist with old patterns for problem solving even when they are not successful.

Confirmation Bias – Tendency to confirm rather than refute a problem's hypothesis even when there is strong evidence that the hypothesis is wrong. Often tend to ignore information that is inconsistent with the hypothesis.

Creative problem solving involves coming up with a solution that is both unusual and useful. Creative thinking usually involves **divergent thinking** or thinking that produces many different correct answers to the same problem or question. Creating a sentence with the word "Springfield" would involve divergent thinking – there is no one specific correct response. A response to the question "What is the capital of Illinois?" would require **convergent thinking** – one correct answer is expected. Convergent thinking does not appear to be related to creativity. Although all creative thought is divergent, not all divergent thought is creative.

Tests (e.g., **Remote Associates Test**) have been developed that measure creativity. Almost all of these tests require divergent thinking. In general, these tests of creativity have not been good at predicting who will be creative in real-life problem solving situations.

There is a modest correlation between creativity and intelligence. Highly creative people tend to have above average intelligence, but not always. Furthermore, having a high IQ does not necessarily mean that someone is creative.

8.5 Decision Making

Decision making requires you to make a choice about the likelihood of uncertain events. Although most of us try to be systematic and rational in making decisions, we do not always live up to these goals. We often lack clear rules about how to make the best decision. Similar to other cognitive tasks, decision making requires us to combine, manipulate, and transform our stored knowledge.

When we have no procedures to use in decision making, we tend to rely on heuristics that include availability, representativeness, and anchoring.

The **availability heuristic** involves judging the probability of an event by how easily examples of the event come to mind. This can lead to bad decision making when the probability of the mentally available events does not equal the actual probability of their occurrence. For instance, in deciding whether one should drive after consuming alcohol, one could decide that this would be a safe thing to do because nothing bad happened the two previous times driving occurred after alcohol consumption.

The **representativeness heuristic** occurs when you decide whether the sample you are judging matches the appropriate prototype. This is probably the most important decision making heuristic, and it usually leads to the correct choice. Decisions concerning diagnosing an illness are often based on the representativeness heuristic — that is, judging how similar the symptoms are to those of the specific disease.

An **anchoring heuristic** occurs when you estimate an event's probability of occurrence and then make adjustments to that estimate based on additional information. We tend, however, to make adjustments that are too small. For instance, you ran out of drinks at your last party. In deciding how many drinks to buy for this year's party, your estimate will probably be based on how many drinks you bought last time and how early into the party these drinks ran out.

The **additive model** is another method for decision making. It occurs when we rate the attributes of each alternative and then select the alternative that has the highest sum of ratings. Additive strategies for decision making are examples of compensatory models. **Compensatory models** allow attractive attributes to compensate for unattractive attributes. **Noncompensatory decision models** do not allow some attributes to compensate for others. One bad rating results in eliminating that alternative.

Decisions can also be made by **elimination of negative aspects** whereby less attractive alternatives are gradually eliminated. Alternatives are eliminated until there is only one that satisfies all the necessary criteria.

Problem Solving Example:

 Describe and give an example of each of the following types of problems: simple, conceptual, and reasoning.

Simple problems, sometimes called "one-shot" problems, are those whose solutions are arrived at through a relatively small number of uncomplicated steps. At the outset the person receives all the information he needs to solve the problem in the form of written or spoken instructions. A simple problem has a specific solution that the person, upon arriving at, usually recognizes as correct.

There are various types of simple problems. The majority of them, such as anagrams, rely on language skills for their solutions. Other simple problems depend on perceptual organization. For example, in the following problem a person might be asked to move only three matchsticks to convert the figure into a 16 match arrangement of four squares. The problem requires that the solver utilize his visual imagery.

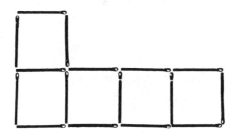

The most sophisticated types of problems require reasoning and logical analysis. A syllogism, for example, requires the use of logic. Syllogisms are three-step arguments that consist of two premises, both assumed to be true, and a conclusion. The problem is to decide whether the conclusion follows logically from the premises. The following is a syllogism:

A=B, B=C

Therefore, A = C   True or false?

Syllogisms are solved with the rules of formal logic. These rules, used in the analysis of arguments, determine whether or not the statement is internally consistent. The formal logic utilized in solving syllogisms requires three things: each premise must be considered with all its possible meanings, all the meanings of the premises should be combined in all possible ways, and the conclusion is valid only if it can be applied to every possible combination of the premises.

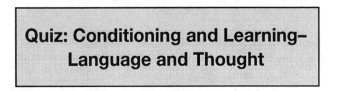

Quiz: Conditioning and Learning– Language and Thought

1. You give a dog a biscuit after every third time he sits. This type of reinforcement is referred to as a

    (A) fixed ratio schedule.

    (B) variable ratio schedule.

    (C) fixed interval schedule.

    (D) variable interval schedule.

2. _____ reasoning involves reasoning from the specific to the general; _____ reasoning involves reasoning from the general to the specific.

   (A) Deductive; inductive

   (B) Inductive; deductive

   (C) Deductive; logical

   (D) Inductive; analogous

3. The most famous classical conditioning study using a human subject was conducted by

   (A) Ivan Pavlov.

   (B) John Watson.

   (C) Albert Bandura.

   (D) B.F. Skinner.

4. Classic research on observational learning which included researchers observing children watching and imitating an adult's aggressive behavior toward a Bobo doll was conducted by

   (A) Ivan Pavlov.

   (B) John Watson.

   (C) Albert Bandura.

   (D) B.F. Skinner.

5.   Forward pairing occurs when

(A)   CS is presented before UCS.

(B)   UCS is presented before CS.

(C)   CS is presented before or after UCS.

(D)   CR is presented before UCS.

6.   The deepest level of processing information appears to be

(A)   phonemic.

(B)   semantic.

(C)   structural.

(D)   No level appears to be deepest.

7.   Once information enters short-term memory, it usually remains there for about

(A)   20 to 30 seconds.

(B)   one minute.

(C)   two minutes.

(D)   five to ten minutes.

8.   Remembering how to ride a bike is an example of

(A)   eidetic memory.

(B)   episodic memory.

(C)   procedural memory.

(D)   declarative memory.

9. The first to plot a forgetting curve was/were

   (A) Fergus Craik and Robert Lockhart.

   (B) Richard Atkinson and Richard Shiffrin.

   (C) George Sperling.

   (D) HermannEbbinghaus.

10. The smallest units of sound that affect the meaning of speech are

   (A) morphemes

   (B) words.

   (C) phonemes.

   (D) phonetics.

ANSWER KEY

1.	(A)	6.	(B)
2.	(B)	7.	(A)
3.	(B)	8.	(C)
4.	(C)	9.	(D)
5.	(A)	10.	(C)

Available at your local bookstore or order directly from us by sending in coupon below.

MAXnotes®

REA's Literature Study Guides

MAXnotes® are student-friendly. They offer a fresh look at masterpieces of literature, presented in a lively and interesting fashion. **MAXnotes®** offer the essentials of what you should know about the work, including outlines, explanations and discussions of the plot, character lists, analyses, and historical context. **MAXnotes®** are designed to help you think independently about literary works by raising various issues and thought-provoking ideas and questions. Written by literary experts who currently teach the subject, **MAXnotes®** enhance your understanding and enjoyment of the work.

Available **MAXnotes®** include the following:

Absalom, Absalom!
The Aeneid of Virgil
Animal Farm
Antony and Cleopatra
As I Lay Dying
As You Like It
The Autobiography of
    Malcolm X
The Awakening
Beloved
Beowulf
Billy Budd
The Bluest Eye, A Novel
Brave New World
The Canterbury Tales
The Catcher in the Rye
The Color Purple
The Crucible
Death in Venice
Death of a Salesman
Dickens Dictionary
The Divine Comedy I: Inferno
Dubliners
The Edible Woman
Emma
Euripides' Medea & Electra
Frankenstein
Gone with the Wind
The Grapes of Wrath
Great Expectations
The Great Gatsby
Gulliver's Travels
Handmaid's Tale
Hamlet
Hard Times
Heart of Darkness

Henry IV, Part I
Henry V
The House on Mango Street
Huckleberry Finn
I Know Why the Caged
    Bird Sings
The Iliad
Invisible Man
Jane Eyre
Jazz
The Joy Luck Club
Jude the Obscure
Julius Caesar
King Lear
Leaves of Grass
Les Misérables
Lord of the Flies
Macbeth
The Merchant of Venice
Metamorphoses of Ovid
Metamorphosis
Middlemarch
A Midsummer Night's Dream
Moby-Dick
Moll Flanders
Mrs. Dalloway
Much Ado About Nothing
Mules and Men
My Antonia
Native Son
1984
The Odyssey
Oedipus Trilogy
Of Mice and Men
On the Road

Othello
Paradise
Paradise Lost
A Passage to India
Plato's Republic
Portrait of a Lady
A Portrait of the Artist
    as a Young Man
Pride and Prejudice
A Raisin in the Sun
Richard II
Romeo and Juliet
The Scarlet Letter
Sir Gawain and the
    Green Knight
Slaughterhouse-Five
Song of Solomon
The Sound and the Fury
The Stranger
Sula
The Sun Also Rises
A Tale of Two Cities
The Taming of the Shrew
Tar Baby
The Tempest
Tess of the D'Urbervilles
Their Eyes Were Watching God
Things Fall Apart
To Kill a Mockingbird
To the Lighthouse
Twelfth Night
Uncle Tom's Cabin
Waiting for Godot
Wuthering Heights
Guide to Literary Terms

RESEARCH & EDUCATION ASSOCIATION
61 Ethel Road W. • Piscataway, New Jersey 08854
Phone: (732) 819-8880   **website: www.rea.com**

Please send me more information about MAXnotes®.

Name _____

Address _____

City _____ State _____ Zip _____

REA's **Problem Solvers**

The "PROBLEM SOLVERS" are comprehensive supplemental text-books designed to save time in finding solutions to problems. Each "PROBLEM SOLVER" is the first of its kind ever produced in its field. It is the product of a massive effort to illustrate almost any imaginable problem in exceptional depth, detail, and clarity. Each problem is worked out in detail with a step-by-step solution, and the problems are arranged in order of complexity from elementary to advanced. Each book is fully indexed for locating problems rapidly.

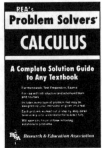

ACCOUNTING
ADVANCED CALCULUS
ALGEBRA & TRIGONOMETRY
AUTOMATIC CONTROL
   SYSTEMS/ROBOTICS
BIOLOGY
BUSINESS, ACCOUNTING, & FINANCE
CALCULUS
CHEMISTRY
COMPLEX VARIABLES
DIFFERENTIAL EQUATIONS
ECONOMICS
ELECTRICAL MACHINES
ELECTRIC CIRCUITS
ELECTROMAGNETICS
ELECTRONIC COMMUNICATIONS
ELECTRONICS
FINITE & DISCRETE MATH
FLUID MECHANICS/DYNAMICS
GENETICS
GEOMETRY
HEAT TRANSFER

LINEAR ALGEBRA
MACHINE DESIGN
MATHEMATICS for ENGINEERS
MECHANICS
NUMERICAL ANALYSIS
OPERATIONS RESEARCH
OPTICS
ORGANIC CHEMISTRY
PHYSICAL CHEMISTRY
PHYSICS
PRE-CALCULUS
PROBABILITY
PSYCHOLOGY
STATISTICS
STRENGTH OF MATERIALS &
   MECHANICS OF SOLIDS
TECHNICAL DESIGN GRAPHICS
THERMODYNAMICS
TOPOLOGY
TRANSPORT PHENOMENA
VECTOR ANALYSIS

*If you would like more information about any of these books,
complete the coupon below and return it to us or visit your local bookstore.*

RESEARCH & EDUCATION ASSOCIATION
61 Ethel Road W. • Piscataway, New Jersey 08854
Phone: (732) 819-8880   **website: www.rea.com**

Please send me more information about your Problem Solver books

Name _____

Address _____

City _____ State _____ Zip _____

"The ESSENTIALS" of Math & Science

Each book in the ESSENTIALS series offers all essential information of the field it covers. It summarizes what every textbook in the particular field must include, and is designed to help students in preparing for exams and doing homework. The ESSENTIALS are excellent supplements to any class text.

The ESSENTIALS are complete and concise with quick access to needed information. They serve as a handy reference source at all times. The ESSENTIALS are prepared with REA's customary concern for high professional quality and student needs.

Available in the following titles:

Advanced Calculus I & II
Algebra & Trigonometry I & II
Anatomy & Physiology
Anthropology
Astronomy
Automatic Control Systems /
   Robotics I & II
Biology I & II
Boolean Algebra
Calculus I, II, & III
Chemistry
Complex Variables I & II
Computer Science I & II
Data Structures I & II
Differential Equations I & II
Electric Circuits I & II
Electromagnetics I & II

Electronics I & II
Electronic Communications I & II
Fluid Mechanics /
   Dynamics I & II
Fourier Analysis
Geometry I & II
Group Theory I & II
Heat Transfer I & II
LaPlace Transforms
Linear Algebra
Math for Computer Applications
Math for Engineers I & II
Math Made Nice-n-Easy Series
Mechanics I, II, & III
Microbiology
Modern Algebra
Molecular Structures of Life

Numerical Analysis I & II
Organic Chemistry I & II
Physical Chemistry I & II
Physics I & II
Pre-Calculus
Probability
Psychology I & II
Real Variables
Set Theory
Sociology
Statistics I & II
Strength of Materials &
   Mechanics of Solids I & II
Thermodynamics I & II
Topology
Transport Phenomena I & II
Vector Analysis

*If you would like more information about any of these books,
complete the coupon below and return it to us or visit your local bookstore.*

The High School Tutors®

The **HIGH SCHOOL TUTOR** series is based on the same principle as the more comprehensive **PROBLEM SOLVERS**, but is specifically designed to meet the needs of high school students. REA has revised all the books in this series to include expanded review sections and new material. This makes the books even more effective in helping students to cope with these difficult high school subjects.

If you would like more information about any of these books,
complete the coupon below and return it to us or go to your local bookstore.